THE BREATH OF THE MYSTIC

by

George A. Maloney, S.J.

DIMENSION BOOKS

Denville, New Jersey

Published by Dimension Books, Inc.
Denville, New Jersey 07834

Copyright © 1974 by George A. Maloney, S.J.

TABLE OF CONTENTS

INTRODUCTION

God was meant to be man's breath. Man was to be healthy and full of life by breathing in the loving power of God. But man polluted his interior environment. What we see around us in the pollution of the air, the streams, rivers, lakes, and oceans, our woods and forests and countryside, and in the jungles of our cities, is but an *icon*, a dramatic image, externalized, of what man is doing within himself in the unlimited expanses of his "inner space." There he was meant to run, fly, soar, with the speed of light; no space, no time would hold him back as he was propelled into the future by the created energy of love, bubbling forth from his center. Instead, he sits now lonely within himself, sick and afraid.

George Harrison of Beatles fame interpreted the modern mood in his song, "Within You and Without You":

> We were talking about the love that's gone so cold
> and the people who gain the world but lose their soul.
> They don't know—they can't see—are you one of them?
> When you've seen beyond yourself then you may find
> peace of mind is waiting there.
> And the time will come when you see
> We're all one and life flows on within you or without you.

Decades before, G. M. Hopkins declared that the world of signs is "here, and but the beholder / wanting." Still, in spite of man's failures, "there lives the dearest freshness deep down things."

Julian Green puts it succinctly: "God is dying of coldness. He knocks on all the doors, but whoever opens? The room is taken. By whom? By ourselves." [1]

Yet we are witnessing a tremendous surge, especially among the young, towards mysticism. Starved for an immediate experience in the deepest reaches of their consciousness, they turn on to the Absolute with a frenetic vengeance that at times reaches pathetic proportion. This explains the fascination among the young for Hindu Yoga, Zen Buddhism, the Tibetan Book of the Dead, Gurdieff, occultism, Edgar Cayce, etc.

Carl G. Jung has pointed out that the impoverished West has lost myths and symbols, the archetypal models implanted in man's subconsciousness whereby he can commune with the invisible world of the Transcendent Absolute. In a dehumanized, rationalistic world, man is rich in techniques, poor in intuitions, in feminine receptivity to the inner voice that resides in the "temple invisible." The reaction—to become a person and to continue to grow into greater personalism through intermutality in an I-Thou relationship—has opened to Western man a great interest in body integration, a growing hunger for solitude and silence, as well as the practice of Yoga and Zen methods of transcendental meditation. From Eastern Christianity there is a new-felt influence upon the youth through the beautiful Byzantine icons, the Jesus Prayer, and the haunting Liturgies that lead a worshiper into a deep experience of God through vivid sense impressions, not the least of which flow from stirring religious music.

TOWARDS AN UNDERSTANDING OF MYSTICISM

Mysticism is one of those often misunderstood words in English usage. Ask the ordinary person on the street what mysticism connotes to him, and he would probably describe something touching demonology, occultism, or magic. Or else the word will conjure up the psychical experiences that nuns and monks of all religions have when they push themselves too far in their fastings and vigils and morbid introspection.

To call a person "mystical" is usually taken to mean that he is a bit "out of it." He cannot be trusted with a wrench or screwdriver, or with any serious task in this "nitty-gritty" world of ours. He is a poetic type, living in a dream world.

Yet in the Far East and in the Christian East of the Greek and Slavic world, mysticism is synonymous with being in touch with the "really real." Reality abides not in the changing, in the temporal, but in the unfathomable abyss where God speaks within the heart of man in silence. Mysticism is a living experience of God, not as an object outside of us, but as an encompassing power of permeating love that, as St. Augustine said, is more intimate to me than I to myself. At the center of our deepest awareness, beyond our habitual pre-conditioning of sense and emotional and intellectual responses, we are gradually purified of our false ego-orientation in order to open ourselves towards the Allness of God.

This openness is attained in a gradual process of communion that unfolds in the ever-deepening silencing of our own inordinate desires and sense of independence and in the surrendering of ourselves to His divine will. It is what must be experienced, not what can be described in words

that is important. Kahlil Gibran has beautifully expressed
the spirit of Eastern mysticism and of all authentic
mysticism in these words:

> It is enough that you enter the temple invisible.
> I cannot teach you how to pray in words.
> God listens not to your words save when He Himself utters
> them through your lips.
> And I cannot teach you the prayer of the seas and the
> forests and the mountains.
> But you who are born of the mountains and the forests
> and the seas hear them saying in silence,
> 'Our God, who are our winged self, it is thy will
> in us that willeth.
> It is thy desire in us that desireth.
> It is thy urge in us that would turn our nights,
> which are thine, into days which are thine also.
> We cannot ask thee for aught, for thou knowest
> our needs before they are born in us:
> Thou are our need and in giving us more of thyself
> thou givest us all. [2]

Mysticism moves beyond the Cartesian duality of
subject and object in order to experience God as the very
inner force within us and all around us, supporting all
being in his mighty, transcendent creativity. Evelyn Underhill has given us an apt description of mysticism that
adequately summarizes what has thus far been said:

> Mysticism is the expression of the innate yearning of the
> human spirit towards total harmony with the transcendent-
> al order, whatever may be the theological formula in which
> this order is expressed. This yearning with the great mystics
> gradually takes possession of the whole field of consciousness;
> it dominates their whole life and attains its climax in that
> experience called mystic union, whether it be with God of
> Christianity, the World soul of pantheism or the Absolute of

philosophy. This desire for union and straining towards it in as much as they are vital and real (not purely speculative) constitute the real subject of mysticism. Through this the human consciousness reaches its further and richest development. [3]

Thus intrinsic to any authentic mysticism is a conscious, immediate communion of the soul with the Transcendent Source of all being. This communion is progressively felt to be a union through assimilation, a continued surrendering of the one possessed to the loving power of the possessor. It is a leaving behind of the operations of the senses, emotions, and intellectual powers in order to "strain upwards in unknowing as far as may be towards the union with Him who is above all being and knowledge. For by unceasing and absolute withdrawal from thyself and all things in purity, abandon all and set free from all, thou will be borne up to the ray of the divine Darkness that surpasses all being." [4]

THE BREATH OF MAN

Breath is the most important gift God has given to man. When one no longer breathes, a doctor pronounces him dead. Breath is a sign of life. It brings us the life-giving oxygen without which we would shortly suffocate and die.

We can say that our breath is in a way a part of God. He shares His life with us when He continues to breathe into us His breath. "Yahweh God fashioned man of dust from the earth. Then He breathed into his nostrils a breath of life and thus man became a living being" (Gen. 2,7).

Again Job calls us back to the complete dependence of man upon the breath that God gives us: "He holds in His power the soul of every living thing, and the breath of each man's body" (Job 12,10). "I was fashioned out of clay. God's breath it was that made me, the breathing of Shaddai that gave me life" (Job 33,4).

The Psalmist, in the Semitic existentialism of the desert mystic, cries out before God's grandeur reflected in the ordered heavens: "By the word of Yahweh the heavens were made, their whole array by the breath of His mouth" (Ps. 33,6).

Yet we are seeing a powerful message from God being acted out in our physical environment today. With millions of humans scurrying about in our congested cities like frenetic ants, who find it day by day more difficult to breathe, who are developing diseases of the lungs, heart and all parts of the body because of the polluted air, God is telling us that we have forgotten that His Divine Spirit of Love is our true breath. "After saying this, He breathed on them and said: 'Receive the Holy Spirit' " (Jn. 20,22).

Many of us have ceased to breathe spiritually. What spiritual diseases we carry around within us because we are not nourished by the fresh Breath of God's Spirit!

Ezekiel was touched by God; His Spirit carried him away and set him down in the middle of a valley, full of bones. There he saw vast quantities of bones lying on the ground, the whole length of the valley, "quite dried up." Then Yahweh told him: "Prophesy over these bones. Say, 'Dry bones, hear the word of Yahweh. The Lord Yahweh says this to these bones: I am now going to make the breath enter you and you will live. I shall put sinews on you, I shall make flesh grow on you, I shall cover you with skin and give you breath, and you will live; and you will learn that I am Yahweh.' I prophesied as I had been ordered. While I was prophesying, there was a noise, a sound of clattering; and flesh was growing on them and skin was covering them, but there was no breath in them. He said to me, 'Prophesy to the breath; prophesy, son of man. Say to the breath, 'The Lord Yahweh says this: Come from the four winds, breath; breathe on these dead; let them live!' I prophesied as He had ordered me, and the breath entered them; they came to life again and stood upon their feet, a great, an immense army" (Ezek. 37:2-10).

GOD'S BREATH: THE HOLY SPIRIT

God's Breath, the Holy Spirit, is truly breathing mightily throughout the world. Men, women, and children are breathing a new life in the Spirit. As a dead man come back to life hungers for food and drink, so a multitude sits in the desert in solitary and communal prayer, hungering for the Living Bread from Heaven.

Prayer is man in his hunger stretching forth in the totality of his being to touch God, his source of life. Prayer is man, having experienced his exile, his poverty and alienation, his sickness and close-to-death condition, crying out that the Giver of life come and heal him deeply. Prayer is man, lonely and afraid, seeking to be accepted by Love so that he may love all mankind in return.

What has caused this hunger for prayer among us today? One reason is that our whole being, made for God, has been frustrated by a steady diet of cotton-candy and now, by His absence, God is making himself powerfully felt. Breath, in so much pollution, makes us stagger frantically towards pure air.

MEANING IN ABSURDITY

Our modern arts are a good index of what has been happening in our world today. In theater, painting, sculpturing, music, dancing, and singing, we encounter a violent rebellion against static, "clear and distinct" Cartesian forms. The 60's saw on stage a Dionysian frenzy of sensation in the whole gamut from topless to bottomless to nude. The "Living Theater" and the "Open Theater" had actors running all over the theater advocating wild freedom and animal license as a reaction to an outdated Puritan type of morality. [5]

Reality as seen by a "realistic" scientific age was really not where it was at! A world that was based on science and reason had produced a comfortable "box" in which modern man could live, like a pre-programmed guinea pig in a laboratory. But what happened to man's power to love strongly, to his basic emotions, appetites starved for individual, spontaneous expression?

In all art forms today, in protest to an ordered universe, we find the accent, not on reasoned reality, but on the absurd, the meaningless, the inexplicable quality that makes up most of our lives. Strinberg, Jarry, Pirandello, Artaud, Ionesco, Beckett and, to a bizarre degree, Genet, have created the "theater of the absurd." Are they telling us life is absurd? Or are their attempts to portray the absurdity in life reactions to a de-humanized rationalism, the land of Swift's *Laputa*? Does reaction not come before the solution or at least before the attempted synthesis? Is there no other alternate than the either/or of rationalism vs. irrationalism?

RETURN TO THE DESERT

But John the Baptist is again raising his piercing cry in the desert. When we turn within and descend into our deeper selves, beyond the habitual, pre-conditioning of our sense, emotional and intellectual baggage, we hear the voice calling for a change of heart, a *metanoia.*

We are temples of the God who lives within us. "Didn't you realize you were God's temple and that the Spirit of God was living among you? If anybody should destroy the temple of God, God will destroy him, because the temple of God is sacred; and you are that temple" (1 Cor. 3:16-17). No wonder Jesus Christ flashed such anger as He cleared the temple that was to be God's place of prayer but had been turned into a den of thieves. "Your body, you know, is the temple of the Holy Spirit, who is in you since you received Him from God. You are not your own property; you have been bought and paid for. That is why you should use your body for the glory of God" (1 Cor. 6:19-20).

If we are temples of the Holy Spirit, then He lives and breathes in us. When we turn within to listen to that breath breathing in us, then we become true temples of prayer.

The heart, in all Eastern religions, including Eastern Christianity, has always been the interior "place," the *locus Dei,* where man meets God. Against a de-personalized highly-scientific culture, modern man seeks freedom to be his true self. Ultimately, true freedom that leads man into love, peace, and joy, the fruits of the Breath of God within us (Gal. 5,22), does not consist primarily in the choice between good and evil, purity and fornication, love and hatred, but consists in man's ability more perfectly to determine himself, in ever-increasing, total consciousness, to be the person God his Maker intends him to be.

More and more, modern man realizes that he must find a center if his existence is to have any meaning. He must be directed towards a goal, one that lies beyond himself, in Another, that is both the source of his existence and the end for which he exists. But today man will not be told in scientific language that this is so. As always in the history of man, he will be as *real* (and as human) as his experience of God is real to him.

To be experienced, God must become present to man. But His presence is a loving presence. If God is the fullness of man's inner cravings, and love is ultimately what all men seek in life, then God must be experienced as a real presence by His loving action within us.

Experiencing God as love can be done in solitude, in a deep I-Thou relation; or in a self-sacrificing love-relationship with another person; or finally through a shared love in a group, a living community. Forgetting one's self, a conversion of the heart or man's turning away from his habitual selfish values towards another in love, necessitate a certain amount of the death process that the interior desert alone can teach us.

But the desert is not the end of man's wanderings. He is heading through the experience in the desert toward the Promised Land. "Heaven is within," said Jesus Christ. Prayer is indeed a purification, an enlightenment where we discard our false delusions. But prayer also is a resurrection, a rebirth, a re-creating process into the New Man.

MYSTICAL PRAYER

There are all too many books written on prayer. I hope this will not be thought of as one "about" prayer. It would defeat its own basic tenet: prayer has been all too often taught us as a technique, a thing we do before God.

I think there is a need for a book of insights that present prayer as a state of existence, rather than an action. It is man standing before God in as great a consciousness as man can possess of the awesome, transcendent holiness of God and of his own utter poverty and lack of completeness. He then surrenders himself to God's love, returning gift for gift received, seeking to serve a loving Father.

I have been bold enough to use in the title of this book the word, "mystic." This was no inference on my part that any of the material here presented is autobiographical! Several points were intended in such a choice of title. The first is that all humans are called to be mystics. Therefore this book is intended for all persons regardless of where they stand in the progress of prayer. In the language of the Greek Fathers (who found this term in St. Paul) the inner life of encounter with the saving, healing power of Jesus Lord was the life of the "Mysteries," of what we call today the Sacraments. Mysteries indicated for the early Christians the "really real" world. It did not mean scorning the world of matter, bread, water, wine, oil, saliva, but it meant seeing through the material signs into a world transfigured by the Divine Logos who was en-fleshed as the Living Mystery and was rendered present to our religious consciousness through material signs and symbols.

Thus the mystic is simply a person who meets God in an ever deepening openness to the "Living Mystery" within him. The mystic is the one who consciously lets the Breath of God breathe in him. He is, as St. Irenaeus says, "The glory of God—a man living to the fullest." The mystic is the person always becoming more *human* as the Holy Spirit divinizes the powers placed in man when God made him "according to the Image and Likeness" of God. A fully realized human being has to be a mystic in the truest sense. We must therefore not limit our understanding of mysticism to the aberrations that accompanied the prayer life of the great saints.

A RETURN TO THE GREEK FATHERS

The early Fathers who articulated a theological doctrine of man were mystics, deep contemplatives. All of them had known the rigorism of a long desert discipline. All hungered passionately for greater union in contemplation with God.

This book, therefore, draws its inspiration and content basically from the early Fathers of the desert, the Greek Fathers who articulated the prayer experienced as "theologians" and the Hesychastic Fathers of the school of the prayer of the heart or the Jesus Prayer.

But it is not a compendium of their doctrine or insights. I humbly offer the reader what I believe are insights that Eastern Christianity gives us as a relevant teaching for today. Thus there is at work both my own intellectual as well as personal, spiritual interpretation, at the risk of seeming somewhat presumptuous in presenting such insights through the prism of my own prayer experience. Let me rather present these as sparks that hopefully will ignite something in the hearts of the reader deeper than the initial insight that formulated them.

1

Prayer As Listening

Basic to the Judaeo-Christian message is the affirmation that God is a living, loving God. In His unique love for each one of us, He communicates with us by giving Himself to us. The fundamental attitude of every Christian is that of listening to God as He communicates Himself through His Divine Word.

The Greeks *looked* upon their gods. But Moses *heard* the almighty, transcendent Yahweh as a voice in the burning bush and on Mount Sinai. God speaks in the quiet of our hearts and we hear Him only when we silence the noise of our selfish desires.

Elijah was told by God to stand on the mountain before Yahweh.

> Then Yahweh Himself went by. There came a mighty wind, so strong it tore the mountains and shattered the rocks before Yahweh. But Yahweh was not in the wind. After the wind came an earthquake. But Yahweh was not in the earthquake. After the earthquake came a fire. But Yahweh was not in the fire. And after the fire there came the sound of a gentle breeze. And when Elijah heard this, he covered his face with his cloak and went out and stood at the entrance of the cave (I Kings, 19:11-13).

The Christian therefore waits in awful expectancy for the Lord to reveal Himself. No one can force himself upon the Lord. The Christian must learn to be utter receptivity, waiting for the Lord to come in His good time and as He wishes to reveal Himself. We must learn the art of arts; to pray is to listen to God. As the Lord drew His beloved disciples aside and spoke to them about matters that the crowds could not have understood, so He beckons us to come aside and be still.

CHRISTIAN HESYCHASM

Christian spirituality first developed as a practical, not a theoretical science, as a life lived in Christ. The early disciples had experienced Jesus Christ, the God-Man, as the Event in their lives. The living Word of God, the Speech of God, became incarnate and spoke to humans about the life that He came to bring us. This fact was the unbelievably Good News, the miracle that Irenaeus and after him all the early Greek Fathers summarized as the purpose of the Incarnation: "God became man that man might become God." The early Christians believed and lived their faith in simple obedience to the Logos Incarnate who spoke through His Church and through the Church's written word about Him.

Jules Lebreton speaks of this first period of the Church's life as characterized by the "directness of a simple, robust soul that has given itself totally to God with its whole heart and all of its thought." At the center of the Christian's life was Christ. Faith was the germ of life; to preach the Gospel was to sow the word of life that had been heard in deep prayer. The new life was given in Baptism and was conceived as life "in Christ," with Christ as the life-giver. The sacraments were "carriers" of Divine Life.

The early Christians in whom Jesus Christ dwelt with His own divine life were called by St. Ignatius of Antioch "vehicles of Christ" (Christophoroi), "carriers of God Himself" (Theophoroi). The true disciple of Christ loved his Master to the extent of being constantly ready and eager to sacrifice even his life for the Lord. "No greater love does man have than to lay down his life for his friend." Ignatius of Antioch writes in his letter to the Romans, "Now I begin to be a true disciple, through suffering and martyrdom."

Towards the end of the 4th century, after the Roman emperors have become Christians and when martyrs no longer shed their blood in witness to their faith and love for Christ, a strange phenomenon occurs in Egypt. Prior to Constantine's edict of toleration, the pagan world fought to eliminate the Christian by martyrdom. Now it is the hermit who takes up the attack and eliminates the world from his being. The dominant tone is aggression. The darkened prison where Christians wasted away, the amphitheaters where voracious beasts tore the martyrs apart, are replaced by the immense desert. For these "athletes of Christ," the desert is the twilight zone between the profane world that groaned under the bondage of sin or chaotic disorientation from God and the heavenly Jerusalem of the transfigured world to come.

These early monastic fathers did not run away from the world as cowards or spiritual egoists, but rather as conscious co-creators, fighters at the most advanced outposts, "men intoxicated with God" as Macarius calls them. They were eschatological pilgrims and prophets, building a community, a pilgrim people of God, a way of life with God in the desert that would resemble most closely the life to come in the *eschaton.* Though living in a

body in time and space, the monk pointed to a transfigured, spiritual existence outside of time and space. We are
told by Palladius in his *Lausaic History* that thousands of
men and women left the cities to build large communities
according to St. Paul's "New Creation" throughout all of
Egypt, Syria and Mesopotamia.

There these Christian athletes sat day and night
before the Lord of the universe and listened to the Word
of God as He sent down upon the arid desert His life-giving
Spirit of love. The fierceness of their asceticism, their
vigils, fastings, mortifications, and constant prayer attest
to their seriousness in listening to the Word of God, for
they knew that unless the heart is silenced from the
demands of self-love, God could not communicate His
living Word to them.

The spirituality of the Fathers of the desert shouts
out to us the terrible jealousy of God who, after giving
Himself, asks all in return from men. The Fathers of the
desert had met God, person to person. He spoke to them
continually. They responded to His condescending love to
men by a total gift of themselves. Their example points
out to us the ideal of Christianity: "Thou shalt love the
Lord thy God with thy whole heart, with thy whole mind,
with all thy strength."

The arid and burning desert flourished as a "spiritual
meadow." The goal of these ascetics listening to God was
to "recapitulate all things in Christ" as Paul put it, to
return to the state of the first man. By centering their true
self in God, they would fructify the seeds of divinity
placed in them when God decreed to make man according
to His image and likeness. St. Macarius in one of his
homilies says: "When the apostle urges the putting off of
the old man, he means the entire man. He means: have

other eyes than those the man has, another head than his, hands and feet that are no longer his."

The Fathers of the desert were preparing for the development of a Christian culture and society. Corporate mankind could not encounter God by starting from fallen human nature, infected with an autonomous self-centeredness and a basic refusal to open itself to God as its supreme reality. God remains exterior to the individual as well as society to the extent that the passions are interior and self-possessive.

Paradoxically, the ascent toward God begins with a descent into oneself. Charles Peguy summarizes the attitude of the contemplative in the desert in his work, *Eve*:

> You know that God alone gives of Himself,
> And that man's being unceasingly decreases.
> - - - - - - - - - - - -
> And that God's being unceasingly goes back
> To its eternal source and its deep night
> And of itself produces its own growth
> And man's salvation and the world's strength.[1]

The paradox of the desert experience is that man must break through the initial fear of leaving his world of sense and psychic experiences that so easily assures him of his own self-sufficiency, to descend into his true ego and there find God, the Source of his being, speaking His eternal Word in the loving surrender of self-communication through His Spirit of Love.

St. Arsenius the Great has always been considered an example of the perfect hesychast, the Christian who silenced his heart in order to listen to God's Word speak within. Hesychast comes from the Greek word *hesychia* meaning tranquillity or peace. Hesychia is that state in which the Christian through grace and his own intense

asceticism reintegrates his whole being into a single *ego*
that is then placed completely under the direct influence
of God dwelling within him.

Arsenius, as the story is told in the *Lives of the
Fathers,* while still at the imperial court of Constantinople,
prayed to God in these words: "Lord, lead me along a way
of life where I can be saved." A voice said to him:
"Arsenius, flee men and you will be saved." The same
Arsenius, now become a hermit, in this new life of silence
made again his same prayer and heard a voice which said to
him: "Arsenius, flee, keep silence, remain tranquil; these
are the roots of impeccability."

This in brief formed the basis of the hesychastic
spirituality. Those who aspired to attain this most intimate
union with God, revealing Himself in the depths of their
being, had to flee from noise, through both exterior and
interior silence which, in the words of St. Basil, is the
beginning of purity of the heart. St. John Climacus further
defines silence, as "first of all, detachment from concern
with regard to necessary and unnecessary things; secondly,
as assiduous prayer; and thirdly, as the unremitting action
of prayer in the heart."

Prayer of the heart is the unremitting consciousness
of God's abiding presence deep within man. It brings about
the state of tranquility, the quelling of all inordinate
movements and desires, passions and thoughts. The heart,
in scriptural language, is the seat of man's life, of all that
touches him in the depths of his personality: all his
affections, his passions, his desires, the seat of all his
knowledge, his thoughts. It is in his "heart" that man
meets God in an I-Thou relationship.

The Word of God, Paul tells us, is "something alive
and active; it cuts like any double-edged sword but more

finely; it can slip through the place where the soul is divided from the spirit, or joints from the marrow; it can judge the secret emotions and thoughts. No created thing can hide from Him; everything is uncovered and open to the eyes of the One to Whom we must give account of ourselves" (Hebr. 4:12-13). Silence and tranquility are necessary in order that the Christian may hear the Word of God which separates man's human way of judging reality from God's way.

The condition that served as a criterion of one's docility in listening to the Word of God was measured by the Fathers of the desert in terms of resting in the Lord or quieting all inordinate desires. This is the state of "passionate indifference," to use the term of Teilhard de Chardin, whereby the Christian surrenders himself totally to the God dwelling and revealing Himself within the living temple of God.

This state of listening is comparable to the seventh day of rest that the Lord took after His labors of creating the world. It is the new day of rest, the day of the *kairos* time of salvation in which man opted always to do that which most pleased the Heavenly Father.

> The promise of reaching the place of rest he had for them still holds good, and none of you must think that he has come too late for it. We received the Good News exactly as they did; but hearing the message did them no good because they did not share the faith of those who *listened* .... There must still be, therefore, a place of rest reserved for God's people, the seventh-day rest, since to reach the place of rest is to rest after your work as God did after his. We must therefore do everything we can to reach this place of rest, or some of you might copy this example of disobedience and be lost (Hebr. 4:1-11).

A PASSING OVER

Basic to listening to the Word of God in prayer is the ability to pass beyond man's habitual reasoning about God and about man's duties toward God. C. S. Lewis in his *Letters to Malcolm* describes this way of destroying idols and images of God in order to be open to God's fresh revelation. "Only God Himself can let the bucket down into the depths in us. And on the other side, He must constantly work as the iconoclast. Every idea of Him we form, He must in mercy shatter. The most blessed result of prayer would be to rise thinking, 'But I never knew before. I never dreamed. . . .' I suppose it was at such a moment that Thomas of Aquinas said of all of his theology: 'It reminds me of straw.' " 2

The Christian must build within himself the type of cell where solitude reigns and where he can come face to face with himself and with God in utter openness, in utter receptivity and without any preconceived ideas of what Jesus Christ, the Word of the Father, will reveal to him that day. Jesus Christ, the mighty Word that goes forth from the mouth of Yahweh and returns fulfilled, is so ineffable, so beyond any conceptualization that as soon as we think we have understood His message, in that moment we have introduced noise. The moment we settle down like the Israelites with the flesh pots of Egypt and assert that now we know Jesus Christ, then we have lost Him. Pilgrims in the desert cannot afford to settle down in a fixed, secure pattern of knowledge and worship and revelation. God is so overwhelmingly great that no human being can know Him completely. We know Him by not knowing Him, by not limiting God's power to reveal and communicate Himself to us in any way He wishes. He is

love infinite and no one can love Him enough to say that
now he can stop growing in love. Knowing and loving God
means the desert experience of meeting the awesome God
on His own terms. It necessitates a *kenosis*, an emptying,
in order that God may fill the void.

Thomas Merton describes this experience as a higher
kind of listening, not a receptivity to a certain kind of
message, but a general emptying "that waits to realize the
fullness of the message of God within its own apparent
void. The true contemplative. . . .remains empty because
he knows that he can never expect or anticipate the word
that will transform his darkness into light."[3]

This way of listening to the Word is the "apophatic
theology" of the Greek Fathers. It is not a mere negation
of man's ability to comprehend God by his own power of
intellect. It is a positive experience in which we come to
know God by not knowing Him; in our poverty and utter
creatureliness, in our sinfulness and alienation from the
Father, we realize that to know God is beyond our power.
As the Christian develops in contemplation, he realizes
more and more that God must reveal Himself. Man can
only wait in the desert of his nothingness, hoping to
receive God as He wishes to make Himself known.

Not only is this way of knowing by unknowing found
in the tradition of the Eastern Christian mystics, but it is
also the common heritage of all true mystics, both of the
East and the West. In the Hindu Upanishadic literature we
read: "He is not known by him who knows him, not
understood by him who understands. He alone contemplates him who has ceased to contemplate him. In all
knowledge as though by intuition, the wise man finds him.
It is in him alone, the Atman (the breath) that each one is
strong; it is in knowing him alone that one becomes

immortal. . . .Other than thinking, beyond non-thinking, unknown when he is known, recognized only when all has disappeared."

Meister Eckhart has been described by Hans Urs von Balthasar as a "Christian Buddhist." This 14th century Rhenish Dominican was certainly influenced by the apophatic mysticism of Pseudo-Dionysius, the anonymous disciple of St. Gregory of Nyssa. Eckhart writes: "If a person wants to withdraw himself with all his powers internal and external, then he will find himself in a state in which there are no images and no feelings of compulsion in him, and he will therefore stand without any activity internal or external."

In the writings of as orthodox a mystic as Jan Ruysbroeck, the Flemish 14th century writer, we find the same apophatic emptying of thoughts induced by our own reasoning process, in an attentive listening to the Word of God. In his *Mirror of Eternal Salvation*, he writes: "Above the reason in the depths of the intelligence, the simple eye of the contemplative soul is always open. It contemplates and gazes at the light, the Word. With pure gaze, enlightened by the Light itself, eye against eye, mirror against mirror, image against image."[4]

Can we say that the great Spanish mystics of the 16th century as St. John of the Cross and St. Teresa of Avila were under an Eastern influence? Or are we closer to the truth in saying that all genuine mystics of whatever religious creed share in the same experience once the contemplative purifies his "heart" and enters therein to contemplate the inner light?

St. John of the Cross expresses his apophatic mysticism in these terms: "The brighter and purer is the supernatural and divine light, the more it darkens the soul, and the less bright and pure is it, the less dark it is to the soul. Yet this may well be understood if we consider what has been proved. . . .namely, that the brighter and the more manifest in themselves are supernatural things, the darker are they to our understanding."[5]

St. Teresa, with balanced judgment, speaks of the necessity of not stopping our intellectual activity except when God powerfully takes over.

> In mystical theology, of which I spoke before, the understanding ceases from its acts for God suspends it. We must neither imagine nor think that we can of ourselves bring about this suspension. That is, I say, that must not be done nor must we allow the understanding to cease from its acts for in that case we shall be stupid and cold, for when the Lord suspends the understanding and makes it cease from its acts, then he puts before it what astonishes and occupies so that without making any reflection it can understand and comprehend what we could only comprehend in years with all the efforts in the world.[6]

To be led by God into such a darkness of our own powers requires that humility which a pilgrim in the desert learns. He knows he is weak; there are enemies all about him. He cries out to his Lord for mercy and pity. He hungers for the presence of his Lord. But he must learn, as Thomas Merton has so often suggested in his spiritual writings, a sense of poverty and of a "sickness" that ultimately is a healthy sign of a detached pilgrim in journey to the fatherland. "Blessed are the poor in spirit for theirs is the kingdom of heaven." Only when the contemplative enters into a vivid experience of his own utter poverty and sickness, of his incompleteness before his Maker, can he begin to experience something of God's richness.

EXODUS EXPERIENCE

One of the richest and spiritually most profound themes in both the Old and New Testaments is that of the Exodus. Because this theme employs a basic archetypal symbol (the dialectic of a starting point of confinement and lesser development, moving to a separation and then climaxing in a return), it evokes a resonance in the heart of every human being, especially the contemplative. In the Exodus, as interpreted by Christian tradition, not only do the Israelites pass from slavery to full service of Yahweh, after He has delivered them from idolatry and decisively established them as His chosen people, but every Christian constantly undergoes, in prayer, this experience of deliverance, of return. Ernest Renan stated that "Monotheism was born between the vastnesses of the desert floor and the desert sky." For the Christian contemplative the Trinity becomes a living reality through an exodus experience of leaving oneself in order to move, under the power of the Spirit (symbolized in the cloud by day and the pillar of fire by night), into the darkness where God reveals Himself through a new way of knowing. God speaks, but His Word is a living reality, an experience in purified love. He comes to heal us, to give us life that we might have it more abundantly.

He comes to feed us not with manna but with His own life, but first we must hunger after this Living Bread. He is the Rock from which flows living water, sweet and nourishing, but only after we have thirsted for this water. A vivid sense of poverty and sickness within the depths of our being is the sure means of touching the merciful heart of Yahweh. The Bridegroom will come only when the bride of the *Song of Songs* can say: "I will seek him whom my heart loves, . . .I sought but did not find him. . . .Have you seen him whom my heart loves?"

Therefore, essential to the exodus experience is the excruciating sense of absence and separation which builds up within the contemplative those awful searing, burning desires that touch the mighty tender heart of God and promise a coming reunion. St. Gregory built up his mystical theology, especially in his classic *The Life of Moses,* around this simple theme of *epectasis*, using St. Paul's quotation to the Philippians: "I can assure you, my brothers, I am far from thinking that I have already won. All I can say is that I forget the past and I strain ahead for what is still to come; I am racing for the finish, for the prize to which God calls us upwards to receive in Christ Jesus" (Phil. 3:13-14).

The Greek word that St. Paul uses for straining ahead, or stretching forward is *epekteinomenos.* Our English translation is quite weak compared to the original Greek. The Greek prefix, *ep(i)*, implies a dynamic pouncing upon, a feverish possessing of a desired good. The prefix, *ek*, hints at the outward movement that is a hunger for the eluctable, unpossessable God.

To the extent that we experience our poverty and sickness, our hunger for health and life increases. We entertain a constant restlessness and dissatisfaction with the degree of love of God that we have attained for, though we possess Him, yet we experience the anguish of separation that increases all the more our hunger. This is the tension that the desert produces, and without it there is no deep growth in contemplation. St. John of the Cross describes beautifully this longing for greater union with God without Whom he cannot live:

> I live, yet no true life I know
>   And living thus expectantly,
> I die because I do not die.
>   Within myself no life I know
> And without God, I cannot live.

This sense of poverty detaches us from all inordinate clinging to persons or things. It is the purity of heart of the Beatitudes that will guarantee seeing God whom we have desired above all else. Meister Eckhart paraphrases this Beatitude: "To be the proper abode for God and fit for God to act in, a man should also be free from all things and actions, both inwardly and outwardly."

THE PROPHET LISTENS TO THE WORD

Once purified by a vivid sense of the allness of God in His awesome transcendence, the mountain of perfection, and a corresponding sense of his own littleness, the valley of his imperfection, the pilgrim now becomes a true listener and interpreter of the Word of God. A prophet in the Old Testament sense is not primarily one who tells the future, but rather, the *Nabi* was God's representative. Having yielded himself totally to the message of God, he was able to return to men and "re-present" God, make God present to His people. Here we see why the Fathers of the desert believed that the medium must become the message. The prophet of the desert was not only communicating a word, but he himself was assimilated into the living Word of God. Paul said it briefly for all prophets: "I live now, not I, but Christ lives in me" (Gal. 2:20).

God possessed His prophet in the inmost depths of his being. His words, his knowledge were given him by the Spirit of God breathing within him, letting the Word go forth from him. The prophet experienced this Word by which ". . .Yahweh made the heavens, their whole array by the breath of His mouth. . .He spoke and it was created. He commanded, and there it stood" (Ps. 33, 6-8). "A breath from Him, and the waters flow! This is the God who makes His word known to Jacob, gives Israel ruling and decree" (Ps. 147:4-8).

The essential conversion *(metanoia)* offered to the pilgrim-contemplative in the desert is always one that makes him pass from the visible world into the invisible world of the almighty uncreated energies of God as the foundation of all reality, the source of happiness, joy and love. In every prophetic conversion we open ourselves up more and more to the reality of the Divine Persons, and we discover in experiential, God-given knowledge that the Trinity is the plenitude of all things.

The prophet begins to experience a breakdown in the habitual conceptualization of God as an object outside of ourselves, and thus he realizes that God permeates all things with His energies. The *Isha Upanishad* speaks of the All-in-Allness of God that ever abides in the depths of man, so that there remains nowhere inside the prophet where God is not: "Plenitude everywhere; Plenitude there, here. From Plenitude comes forth Plenitude and everywhere one with itself there remains Plenitude."

One of the great Byzantine mystics, St. Symeon the New Theologian (+1022) describes this interpenetration of God in His loving energies within the being of the contemplative:

> Frightful thing in truth, Master, frightful
> beyond all expression,
> that the Light which the world does not possess
> shows itself to me,

that the One who is not within this world loves me
and that I love the One who is nowhere in visible things.
I am seated on my bed, while being beyond the world,
and, while in the middle of my cell, the One
    who is beyond the world,
I see Him present here, I see Him and I speak to Him
and—dare I say it!—I love Him, and He on
    His part loves me,
I eat, I live on this contemplation alone
and, being but one with Him, I pass through the heavens.
That this be true and certain, I know it,
but where then is my body, that is what I do not know.
I know that the One who remains motionless comes down,
I know that the One who remains invisible appears to me;
I know it, the One who is separated from all creation
takes me within Himself and hides me in His arms,
and from then on I am beyond the entire world.
But in my turn, I a mortal, I so
    unimportant in the world,
I contemplate in myself, completely, the
    Creator of the world,
and I know that I shall never die, since
    I am within Life
and that in its fullness I have Life which
    gushes within me.
He is in my heart, He lives in heaven;
He shows Himself equally resplendent here and there.

The life of prayer or contemplation is simply the realization of God's presence in us. He must not be conceived as an object but as the source of our very life's breath. He breathes in our breath, by His loving actions of creation, preservation, sanctification. The prophet in the desert learns by experience that the whole created world has at its interior the 'inscaping' presence of the Trinity. The world is charged with His divine energies, which are working to recreate the world by fulfilling the plan lovingly intended by the Trinity from all eternity. St. James tells us that every good gift is from above and comes down to us from the Father of lights (James 1:17), and hence it behooves us to render Him thanks and adoration. Our poverty fills us with joy in experiencing the great richness of the Father, who begets His children and bestows upon them a universe of manifold beauty and riches. "In Him we live and move and have our being" (Acts 17:28). God is hidden in all of creation, but He reveals Himself to the children who have eyes to see Him everywhere.

Teilhard de Chardin beautifully expresses the vision of the purified prophet of the desert when he writes: "Jesus Christ is shining diaphanously through the whole world for those who have the eyes to see." The presence of God is co-terminous with the whole of being. God is not a being among other beings. He is the source from which all beings exist. He is the "first, and there is no second."

But this same Trinity, the Source breathing His love that begets His Word is, as St. Augustine says, more intimate to me than I to myself. He tells us: "Enter into yourself; it is in the interior man where Truth is found." We inwardly experience the mystery of living in the Trinity, for the Trinity dwells within us. This relation of mutual indwelling blossoms in a continual, loving process of life shared between the Divine Persons and ourselves. The Spirit, as St. Irenaeus says, comes to seize us and give us to the Son and the Son gives us to the Father. Jesus Himself had already spoken His prophetic word: "If anyone loves me, we will come to him and make in him our abode" (Jn. 14,23). Prayer is the awareness of this holy presence, and it is the adoration and completely self-surrendering worship that follow from this awareness.

The experience of God in prayer is the *delectatio victrix*, the conquering taste, that Augustine describes as the only power capable of uprooting the delights of fulfilling our own selfish desires.

In an attitude of profound reverence, adoration and humility, we sit and behold Life itself unfolding within us. The acceptance of our total weakness and our inability to seize God by our own means creates within us an abandonment to the action of the Spirit who allows us to cry out Abba, Father, in a true experience of being wanted and loved by Omnipotence itself. The Spirit makes us realize that, at the heart of matter and of the whole created world, including ourselves, the Trinity lives a mystery of love, the love of three Persons in their reciprocal relationship to each other.

Paul Tillich has expressed, in modern psychological terms of self-actualization, this mystery that each prophet-contemplative begins to experience in prayer. The triadic movement towards self-actualization is a movement of love. God the Father, the Abyss of all potentiality, breathes forth His Spirit of Love, and the Logos becomes the actualized Meaning of God, the potential of God realized through the Spirit, in whom God goes out of Himself and returns to unity through His self-actualization in the Logos, His perfect Image.

The mystic realizes that at the basis of reality is the drive toward that communion or love which exists between persons in mutual self-surrender. Separation is overcome by self-actualization through love. We experience this personal love of God, giving Himself to each one of us through His realized Meaning, the Word, and His unifying force of love, the Spirit, and this experience is what makes us grow in true existence. The contemplative has had the words of St. John authenticated in his prayer: "We ourselves have known and put our faith in God's love towards ourselves. God is love, and anyone who lives in love lives in God, and God lives in him" (I Jn. 4:16).

As we grow in prayer, we realize more and more the complete gratuity of God's great love for us. In this process of growth, God's love and God Himself become for us the Trinity, pouring itself out towards us, creating us anew in a living relationship of loving response to our Creator, the Source of life and love. The prophet listens to the Word of God which tells of His great love for us. St. Paul expresses the Prophetic Word of God in these words:

> Blessed be God the Father of our Lord Jesus Christ, who has blessed us with all the spiritual blessings of heaven in Christ. Before the world was made, He chose us, chose us in Christ, to be holy and spotless and to live through love in His presence, determining that we should become His adopted sons, through Jesus Christ for His own kind purposes to make us praise the glory of His grace, His free gift to us in the Beloved. . .Such is the richness of the grace which He has showered on us in all wisdom and insight. . . .Now you too, in Him, have heard the message of the truth and the good news of your salvation and have believed it; and you too have been stamped with the seal of the Holy Spirit of the Promise, the pledge of our inheritance which brings freedom for those whom God has taken for His own to make His glory praised (Ephes. 1:3-14).

Many Christians wish to preach the Word of God before they have sat before the throne of God and listened to the Word tell us about God's wonderful plan. Americans are especially prone to be doers, performers. We must learn to sit before God and hear of His infinite love for us and His whole creation. Then we will be able to give our prophetic response. With Isaias the Prophet we will be able to answer: "Here I am, send me" (Is. 6;9).

St. Paul again in the Epistle to the Ephesians returns to the amazing love of God for us and the need on our part to realize all that He has done for us. We must learn that it is God's message, not ours, that we are to preach. Paul writes:

> But God loved us with so much love that He was generous with His mercy; when we were dead through our sins, He brought us to life with Christ—it is through grace that you have been saved—and raised us up with Him and gave us a place with Him in Heaven in Christ Jesus. This was to show for all ages to come, through His goodness towards us in Christ Jesus, how infinitely rich He is in grace. Because it is by grace that you have been saved, through faith; not by anything of your own, but by a gift from God; not by anything that you have done, so that nobody can claim the credit. We are God's work of art, created in Christ Jesus to live the good life as from the beginning He had meant us to live it (Ephes. 2;4-10).

Each experience in prayer begins with an act of faith that God has already done so much, done all in loving us and in giving us His Son, Jesus. Thus the Christian learns to relax in the Lord, resting entirely upon Him. The Good News is that God truly loves us. We learn this only by experience, in sitting and listening to the voice of Christ's Spirit present within us.

In the parable of the Prodigal Son, the older son never really fell in love with the Father. He worked for him as a servant would, demanding quid-pro-quo. The Father could never be a Father to him, because the son never let the love of the Father pour over him and change his value-structure. The younger son, however, crushed by his sinfulness and purified by his alienation and separation from his Father, let the Father be his Father. The Father did everything for him and rejoiced to do so.

The desert experience teaches us what the Prodigal Son learned by being a pilgrim, separated from the Father's home and love by his own doing, namely, the desire to be independent of his Father's love. But returning to the Father's home, he becomes docile and supple to the Father's slightest wish. No longer is he under the law of a tyrant, but he is liberated by an experience of forgiving love, so that he can return love for love. The prophet then sits joyfully in the presence of his Father and hears about the great love the Father has for him.

Then that prophetic Word moves us to make our response. We move outward to build a community founded on the same joy and love that we have experienced through the gratuitous love of the Father for His children. Having been accepted in love by God, we have a sense of *real* identity. We can go out as God's representatives and bear witness to this great divine love for all men. The existential Word is being spoken in our daily lives. It is a continuation of the same prophetic Word of Scriptures that lives in our hearts. The Word is revealed in every event of our lives as we experience the Trinity unfolding its self-communication throughout all creation.

The prophet then beholds God's great love in the beautiful smile of a child, in the violence of a storm, in the calm serenity of a moonbathed lake, in the suffering body of a dying person. We no longer need to leave the world, for we are now co-creators of that existential Word. As Paul says, with Christ we reconcile the whole universe to the Father. We unite ourselves with others who have heard the Word of God, and we offer ourselves in loving service, within the "phylum of love," the Church. Seated beneath the Tree of life in a new Eden, the contemplative communicates with God in the cool of the evening. He seeks to bring the whole of creation into the full harmony intended by God when He commanded man to order and subjugate the whole sub-human cosmos.

Having returned to the world, the prophet now sees the world through different eyes. He sees it being transfigured slowly by that inner life of God that inhabits men "intoxicated with God," as Macarius described the fathers of the desert. The message of contemplation is clearly this: to the degree that one has purified and disciplined himself to sit before the Lord and to listen to His Word, to that extent he can stand before the world and witness to the Word in loving service. Prayer as listening reveals to us the need to become pilgrims, poor, detached, purified, hungry for God, stretching out to possess the unpossessable that "makes all possession vain." It teaches us the need then to become prophets of the Word; meditating on the Word spoken in Scripture and relived in the mystery of the indwelling Trinity, we are sent forth as witnesses to that same existential Word being spoken in the world, as we yield ourselves to the process of bringing forth that Word in its fullness.

The Mother of God, Mary most pure, will always be the model and the archetype for all Christians who aspire to become contemplatives. She was first a virgin over whom the Spirit hovered. She conceived by the Spirit, and the Word was incarnated within her. Then she became the witness to that Word as she "set out at that time and went as quickly as she could to a town in the hill country of Judah" (Lk. 1;39). She brought forth the Word and gave it to the world through her humble service. "Behold the handmaid of the Lord; be it done unto me according to Thy Word."

2

Growth in Prayer

Anyone serious about prayer sees in his personal life and in the lives of others around him a great crisis in prayer. Activism seems to increase by the day; this peculiar disease which afflicts so many Americans, the itch to be always doing, must be one reason why we find it difficult to be silent and to listen to God speak within us. Our American culture seems to feed us with the principle that man can do anything he sets his mind to do. In the time of St. Augustine this principle was called Pelagianism. When we enter seriously upon an intense following of Jesus Christ, there is much zeal and enthusiasm, and activism dominates even our spiritual life. But we forget that only when we are crushed can God start working. We forget that sanctification is the work of the Spirit; that man can and must dispose himself; but it is God who has to crush us and then build a whole new world upon that dead self

There is also a practical materialism at the root of our way of life, a pragmatism that measures real success by material values. I must see immediately in my work and prayer something concrete or otherwise the work is useless. All this fills me with a sense of great self-sufficiency. That which I undertake for the love of God and neighbor I soon treasure as something that feeds my own importance. I rather like the idea of managing things for God and doing things; and so I move from a state of being before God to a condition of nervously doing things. This builds up an ego separated from God—and a person who is autonomous does not pray. That person may build up an idol of God which is the object of his conversation in prayer. There is a subtle type of pharaisaism that uses God as a static object to give me a feeling of a good conscience, but there is no longer the willingness to take the wild risks of the desert.

But there is also in our modern world a more positive value accounting for a real crisis in prayer. The individual is coming forth as a person. There is now a great need for an "I-Thou," a person-to-person confrontation in prayer that unfortunately did not always exist in our spiritual life. We engaged in a great deal of repetitious, formal prayer, especially in our liturgical and communal prayers. But today the person is important; he feels he must be free, free to say his "yes" to God. I must have a sense of identity if I am to meet God deeply. And so the modern person going to prayer feels the need to get down deeper into his intimate self, into that which the Eastern Christian calls the heart, that complexity which is not just our physical heart but is the totality of our being, standing before God who is the ground of our being, looking up into His face and saying, "yes." This is the type of total prayer that we are searching for today.

The following, familiar example is used to illustrate how we live on different levels of our being: A lake admits of different levels. There is the surface, the rock formation of the lake, the flora, the mud; all are parts of the lake, but these are not quite that which gives to the lake its "lake-ness." That spring bubbling new life into the lake is the source of the lake's being. In man there are the various levels of the senses, emotions, affections, whose reactions often have been predetermined through heredity, education and social conditioning. All are parts of me, the existential I that I am; but still, somehow or other, it is not the real I. But I can go down deeper and deeper into the pit of my being until I hit the bottom. Here I am most free, away from the pre-determinisms of the senses and the emotions, free to have a real confrontation with God in which I say "yes" to Him with my very being and not just my sense life, not just words or pious sentiments flowing out of my emotional life. Even though the "cave" within me be in utter dryness and darkness, yet I call up the whole of my being to respond to God, not once in prayer, but as a continuous state of being. At this moment I become a contemplative, when I become habitually a person of prayer. Prayer is then not so much a thing I do or words I say; it is a state of being in communication with God as the ultimate ground of my total being.

CONSCIOUSNESS OF GOD'S LOVING PRESENCE

In discussing growth in prayer, I would like to avoid the traditional categories deduced from the writings of St. Teresa of Avila: discursive prayer, prayer of affection, of simplicity, of faith, of quiet, of recollection, of full union, of ecstasy and of spiritual marriage. I believe there is a need to treat growth in prayer in a different way, one which is linked with the psychology of self-identity in a conscious relationship with one who loves us. I am not interested in writing a treatise on how the Eastern Fathers conceived prayer. I am more interested in using their insights to present the life of prayer in terms of a process of growth in the consciousness of the abiding presence of God and His ever-increasing activity of love assimilating ourselves into a union with Him that can be called divinization.

What then is contemplation? It is basically a look turned toward God. It is a human being standing, as it were, outside of the habitual idea that he has of himself, the person that he thinks he is. It is his getting down below that false everyday ego and getting into his deepest source where he stands before God, consciously turning toward his Source, his Origin. Here we can see we are not dealing with an exercise of piety alone. We are certainly not dealing with anything that is dependent upon perseverance in a certain method. But contemplation is something applicable to every human being, and therefore should be as natural as a baby looking on his father or mother's face.

This looking upon God is, therefore, the essential act of contemplation. It does not consist in having beautiful thoughts, nor in having any emotions, sentiments, or piety. It consists fundamentally in standing before God, not with one faculty perceiving some facet of God but with man's total being absorbed into the total being of God. It is the return of my whole being back to God as a gift that expresses the attitude which I call worhip-prayer, the ultimate point of contemplation.

It cannot be found in the "give me, give me, Lord," of petition, nor even in thanksgiving nor even expiation or sorrow. But it must ultimately overwhelm us in our praise, because we understand from an experience of being created by God what it means to belong to God, where "God is more intimate to me than I to myself." This experience can come only in contemplation, and no one can reach contemplation with his natural powers alone, because only God can reveal to a person that He is the Source of his being.

Thus contemplation is in the form of a dialogue, but a dialogue on the level of being. It is not just a banal conversation. We could spend long hours talking to God—"I say this and He says that—." This is not contemplation. And you know yourself how you can spend years in this sort of dialogue and it does not perceptibly change your personality. It does not give you an immersion, an assimilation into God where you truly understand that you live, no longer you yourself, but God lives in you. This immersion in God can come only from contemplation, not from a banal conversation with Jesus.

To understand what this kind of dialogue-in-being means, we must go to the dialogue that is taking place constantly, within us and in the world outside us, between the Father and the Son, the Word. God dialogues with His Word, because the Word is the outpouring of the mind of the Father. The Word, as spoken and produced by the Father, is the perfect replica who says everything exactly as the Father does. The Word mirrors forth the mind of God—it is the echo, the spoken thought of God.

So our dialogue with God must participate in some type of intimate ontological relationship that touches the core of our being, not just our intellect, not just emotions or good sentiments, as would a prayer that might be empty of involvement of being. Contemplation involves my *whole* being and changes my life ontologically, bringing about a continuous process of growth. The soul is just a created being that remains the same identical thing, but in the relationship between the creature and God as a Spirit the soul is always growing. Contemplation is the soul's pushing itself outward towards God as the totally Other. In such a state of being the soul grows, and it admits of an infinity of growth. "Eye has not seen, nor ear heard. . .nor has it entered into the mind of man to conceive what God has prepared for those who love Him. . ." (I Cor. 2,9).

One author says that we must look upon God with our 'entrails.' We have to get involved with our total being, otherwise it is not true prayer. We are what we are through a gift from God, but it is a gift that is an ongoing process. We have to understand that God's uncreated energies are within us and are continually creating us. Every time we breathe, God is giving forth His Word in us. And so we want to return this gift by that complete openness to God that looks into His face and says, "Yes, I am at Your service." Love must be proved by deeds and the deed is precisely this attitude of complete service towards the One who first has loved us.

Carl Jung has defined modern man in terms of the *animus* and *anima*—the male, the aggressor, the initiator, the one who begins the love process, and the feminine, the receptor, the one waiting and then returning. Thus the *anima* is not just passive, but it is first a passive waiting and then an active returning of love for Love. So it is also with God Himself. If He is Love, He is not only the aggressive Father who has first loved us, but He is also receptivity. He is also the *anima* who waits upon our return and then joyfully accepts our love. And it is we who create this latter relationship with God. If we do not say yes, the relationship is never realized for all eternity, but when we say yes, it goes on and on, as God wants it to, and it becomes the most intimate love relationship possible. He truly wants us, as St. John says, to be children of God. But that means He wants to create us more and more into His likeness, so that we may know no end of this assimilation and greater growth into the likeness that is complete only in His beloved Son, Jesus Christ. Eternity will not mean the end of this process of growth but will offer further means of serving one another and thus of growing in loving service to the Father of us all. Our heaven depends upon the degree of contemplation, of worship, of true dying to self and rising with Christ in giving ourselves back in glory to God, that we have reached in this life.

Therefore contemplation is my total expression as a creature before my Creator to whom I owe my whole being. It is a gift of my whole being in a total act of surrender that grows daily moment by moment. Gerard Manley Hopkins, S.J., put it pithily in a short poem:

> Thee God I come from,
>   To Thee go.
> All day long I like fountain flow,
>   From Thy hand out,
> Swayed about
>   Mote-like
> In Thy mighty glow.

This is the attitude I would think that Jesus had on the mountain when He prayed all night before the face of His Father. His prayer was the Word issuing forth from the Father and going back as an echo to the mind that uttered that Word.

THE LIFE OF MOSES

If you wish then to start out in search of God along the long, sinuous road of contemplation, you may feel that you are throwing yourself into the pursuit of the unknowable; that all you have in your favor is your great desire to pursue God up the mountain as Moses did. But even this desire has been given you by God. God hides this fact from you; you think at least you can give Him this desire, but even this has come from God.

The important thing now as you begin your journey is to desire to listen to God. You want to know Him deeply as a person, not as a concept. You want to destroy the idol that you have been living under and that you have been calling your God. You want to meet the living God of Abraham, Isaac, and Jacob. But He can only be met in the desert of your own being, in the depths where you encounter God in your dread of loss. So few of us have the courage to discipline ourselves, to cut ourselves off from all the attachments that build up our self-centeredness, to go out into the desert and be at the mercy of God.

Using the beautiful description of St. Gregory of Nyssa in his *Life of Moses,* we set off on this search for God and begin ascending the great mountain. We prepare our bags, we saddle up the donkey and set off on the road. We set off at daybreak and it is a great departure. We are saying goodby. To whom? To what? In a way, to everything and yet, in a way, to nothing. To everything, because we must be pilgrims stripped of all things, and we must let God, the Ground of our being, expose Himself to us as He wishes. And yet we are not cutting ourselves off from anything, because on that donkey we are putting our past history, our intelligence, our imagination, all our weaknesses, our strengths. We are not throwing off this person that we existentially are for some ideal that we would like to be, for some rarified angel. God is going to meet us in the desert of our existential history. And so we take along with us on this road all that we are.

For this entrance into prayer we need solitude and silence, at least sometime during the day or night, in which we can enter deeply into ourselves and find God. And yet today, silence and solitude are rare commodities. Over-reacting in all of our great feverish activity, we behave as though God needs our activity. Surely we need to be involved in giving ourselves to those who need our service; a piety that is self-centered is worthless. But we are losing many of the real values that ought to be in our life, through the lack of some moments of deep solitude and silence each day. Over-absorption in activities makes silence and solitude most difficult and prayer almost impossible.

We are not concerned here with communal or liturgical prayer, but it can be said that if there is this continued, daily personal relationship, not in an egocentric way, but as a God-given encounter, then we will also be able to pray in a communal way and in a liturgical way.

The first step in any deep interior prayer is an act of faith. I cannot stress this too much. Many of us run into prayer, and there is no atmosphere, no composition of place, no *locus Dei*, the place where we are to meet God. Surely God is everywhere, and we enter prayer knowing that God fills all of His creation. We do not want to pin God down nor to reify Him into a concept or a picture. But on the other hand, we need to be localized. We need to gather all of our disparate forces into a point, a still point of concentration. And so when we enter into ourselves in the presence, the conscious presence of God. . .and that is an act of faith. We can be very relaxed. We can let this act of faith pass over our psychosomatic self by perhaps just repeating slowly the word, "God" or "Jesus" or "Lord Jesus Christ, Son of God, have mercy on me, a sinner." We can coordinate this with our breathing by an intake and then an exhalation as we get deeper into ourselves. The rhythm that is basic to our physical life becomes the rhythm of our spiritual life; with each breath there is a thrust toward the transcendent God who is beyond us, and there is that desire to possess the unpossessable within us. Thus our breathing coordinates this basic thirst for God who is beyond us and yet the God who is also within us.

The beginning stage in prayer, as in the unfolding human friendship, is a prayer of simple reflection. When anyone in a friendship starts to know another extrinsically, one does not immediately plumb the depths of the other person until after years of coming to know the person with one's mind and intellect, as well as with senses. Gradually, faith and trust are built up, so that one can admit that person into the inner sanctuary of the other's being.

PRAYER AS REFLECTION

In Christian prayer there is always a need for ordering the truths of faith. We begin with a method of "meditation" that enables us to reflect, ponder, measure, compare, and organize. Here the basic activity revolves around the use of our own intellect and reasoning process on the matters of faith. This movement moves one to affections, towards the union to feel, to touch the spiritual reality about which one is meditating. In a discursive manner, we meditate on the Trinity, but always each mental activity is a preparatory step towards a living experience of the Trinity, not as a concept, but as the Living God abiding within us and communicating Himself to us.

We start with the great mysteries of Scripture—the Prophetic Word. The Bible is the only place to begin, because here we meet the Living Word that has come down from the Father to teach us about Him. "God so loved the world as to give His only Begotten Son" (Jn. 3:16). There is no other way to know God than through the Way, the Truth and the Life that is Jesus Christ. Thus we start with Scripture: a page, a scene from the New or Old Testament. We run through it, reading it, simply stopping where we find some point of reflection. But gradually we move away, even from a construction of this historical moment, to an encounter, a subject-to-subject relationship. The text becomes a sign of the presence of God and the Divine action of God towards us. The things that Jesus Christ said and did, because they are the theandric actions of the God-Man, enter into the area of the *kairos*, the timeless time of God Himself. The important element in our prayer life is that we are encountering God. The where and the when are not as important as *who* it is.

We soon get away from the details, just as the Evangelists did. They really were not too much concerned with the details of when and where, but rather with the great Christ-event. And so our act of faith brings us to the presence of Christ. Here the power of God, the power of Christ's resurrectional presence, begins to work upon us. The same Christ who is alive today begins to work upon us, as we move away from the details of the historical event to the actual event of this Person, Jesus Christ, meeting us now, and the event of our opening ourselves to His activity.

Gradually we find that, as we move into this simple presence of Jesus Christ, there is a great peace and quietude. We find that we are no longer doing things; we are in a state of just being in His presence. We find also that there might be long periods of dryness, where we seem to be getting nowhere. We have nothing with which to measure our progress. But as we did not start from a position of not having to a level of now having, but rather we started from a stage of being to a stage of greater being, we realize that we cannot measure progress in being in the presence of the Lord except by moving out into the world. In contact with God's creation, especially with other intellectual, loving beings, we can test how deeply our being has been "rooted" in the Ultimate.

GROWTH IN SYNTHESIS

We find, as we move out into the world, that the Divine Word becomes a presence surrounding everything and everyone, a power that is acting in all. Everything in a way continues as before. It is the same world that we saw before; but now we seem to be on a new dimension in relation to God and to the world. We begin to see more clearly now, as though we were blind before. Now we have stepped onto a new plateau. Always there is this one single thought that gives us great peace and joy, namely, we find that we are growing in friendship with Christ.

Our prayer has become one of passively resisting any activity that is our own, while at the same time transforming all our activity into the receiving of God's activity. Our thoughts in prayer become very simplified and unified, to the point that God is no longer an object we attain through our activity, but now God is so intimately present to us that in silence and waiting, we *are* in His holy presence. I open myself to God's presence. It is God's activity that I am able to perceive, and, always in the light of a deepening faith, I know that this Person truly loves me, and I trust more deeply in His love. There comes over me a greater peace and assurance, a sense of growing unity with God and with the world. There is no anxiety; only childlike abandonment to the sacrament of the present moment.

A global sense of God's presence develops in us. We know God is guiding us. He is our Father. Christ is our Brother, our Spouse. After months, perhaps even years, the contemplator has a breakthrough in consciousness. It might be looking at a scene of nature, or in prayer, in the midst of doing one's daily work, wherever the person is, he perceives in himself and outside of him, in nature, a presence that becomes like a strong, gentle voice, attracting, drawing him with deep love into a greater union. There is a desire to be even more docile, more silent; an inkling comes over us, a holding of the breath almost, the suspending of all the intellectual powers. To think, reflect becomes almost repugnant, a waste of time. There is only the desire to wait, to breathe in the presence of God that is now so vividly felt everywhere.

Then we know that our prayer has changed and likewise our lives. Joy is the ultimate criterion of the degree of faith since, if we believe that God is present in all events and is loving us and that nothing is impossible to the Lord, then we must be always joyful even in the throes of excruciating purification.

We know now that we have entered into a whole new mode of thinking and feeling. Before, there was knowledge by our own acquisition. Now we understand that it is a whole new way of knowing—by not knowing with our own powers in our human, habitual way, but knowing through receiving God's presence, of allowing His loving activities to operate upon us.

It is not an ordinary repose of the human faculties as such, but we feel that we are emptied of inordinate passions, of our own self-orientation, desires, ambitions, and thoughts.

In this state of growth in prayer, one must avoid conceptualizing this Presence in order to possess it, to carry it wherever one wants and to do with whatever one wishes. This is idolatry and constitutes one of the greatest dangers of contemplatives. To reach this point and then to want to cling to it selfishly, not to be indifferent but to want this state of union for itself: this is to create an idol of God; it is to stifle further growth and to remain on a narcissistic level.

THE DARK NIGHT

In this illumination that can become very intense, there suddenly or gradually appears great darkness. The light now reveals itself in a new modality, appearing as darkness itself. In this light, the more that a soul comprehends God, the more it discovers God is far away. One begins to cry out in the darkness of the night for God. If it were not so dark, if we had not lost our way and had not that feeling of utter alienation from God, we would have settled down to a secured possession of God. We would have said, "How good it is to pitch our tents here." But it is dark and we have to be on our way, seeking the Lord. Thus God leads us further into the dark desert.

As we descend more deeply within ourselves, God reveals our own abyss of nothingness before the Mountain of God that fills us with dread. The more one advances, the more the names of God have no sense; images of Him disappear; nothing satisfies. The very presence of God that once flooded the soul in deep prayer and in contact with the world now seems to be absent. The soul has gone into the full night, the dark desert. Only a person who has felt this friendship, this intimacy with God, knows what the absence of God means. Only the person who has loved knows what absence of the loved one means.

God develops this necessary pruning, this dying of the seed, in order that more fruit can be brought forth. This is a necessary dying to our self-reliance unto a deepening of faith that only can come when we are in this darkness, standing before a wall that is impermeable. We cry out for God to show Himself in the night of the desert where we understand our own absolute nothingness before God. There is a silencing of our own powers like the silence of steel in the black night. Now one has to stand firm and cry out in deep, dark, stark faith for the mercy of God to reveal Himself. "Lord, Jesus Christ, Son of God, have mercy on me, a sinner!"

The sinner moves into that area of dread that Thomas Merton writes about in his book on "The Climate of Monastic Prayer":

> Following Gabriel Marcel, dread divests itself of the sense of possession, of having our being and our power to live, in order that we may simply be in perfect openness, turned inside out, of the defenselessness that is utter simplicity, and total gift. This is at once the heart of meditation and of liturgical sacrifice. It is the sign of the Spirit upon the chosen people of God, not the ones who 'have an inner life' and deserve respect in the gatherings of an institution notorious for piety but have simply surrendered to God in the desert of emptiness where He reveals His unutterable mercy, without condition and without explanation, in the mystery of love. Now we can

understand that full maturity of spiritual life cannot be reached unless we first pass through dread, anguish, trouble, and fear that necessarily accompany the inner crises of spiritual death in which we finally abandon our attachment to our exterior self and surrender ourselves completely to Christ. But when this surrender has been truly made there is no longer place for fear and dread, no doubt or hesitation in the mind of one who is completely and finally resolved to seek nothing and do nothing but what is willed by Him, by God's love.[1]

The night seems very dense and dark, the desert seems very dry and empty. One feels that he will never find God again; and yet there is no true panic or disquietude. There is only a deep abiding trust that God will come; that in a way He is present in His absence. The soul is being called to experience God in a new modality, no longer experiencing Him through one's own concepts or feelings with assuring repercussions in one's physical life, but now nakedly through faith. Faith grows as we come to know God in the unknowable. The soul feels immobile, blocked at the bottom of the mountain, completely alone, crying out to God for His infinite mercy. God is so much the Other. We begin to experience our creatureliness, our poverty, and our utter dependence upon God.

To become a true contemplative, to let God do with us what He wants, demands the greatest suffering. This is the common doctrine of Origen, St. Gregory of Nyssa, Pseudo-Dionysius, Meister Eckhart, St. Teresa of Avila, and St. John of the Cross. These mystics were not neurotic people who took particular delight in suffering for love of God. They had entered into their deepest self where they began to lose the most precious possession that a human being has before he learns to surrender himself in love to the Other, the control of his own little world of reality. When you lose this, you either have to be insane or you are a mystic, completely trusting by faith that God will do whatever He wishes with you. When *He* becomes the center of all reality, then you have moved into true wisdom. And this is contemplation.

"WINTER IS PAST"

God has been preparing for a great meeting through this dryness. Perhaps, suddenly He makes Himself felt in a flashing light that illumines the desert, and all the sweetness that was felt before suddenly is very empty in comparison to the presence of God that is felt now. The desert springs into new life, full of flowers in full bloom.

"Come then, my love, my lovely one, come.
For see, winter is past, the rains are over and gone.
The flowers appear on the earth.
The season of glad sons has come.
The cooing of the turtledove is heard in our land. . .
Come then, my love, my lovely one, come.
My dove, hiding in the clefts of the rock,
In the coverts of the cliff, show me your face.
Let me hear your voice; for your voice is sweet
And your face is beautiful (The Song of Songs: 2;10-14).

One enters into a new world. Solitude is no longer solitude. God appears everywhere in everything. He shows Himself in corners that were before very obscure. Now everything is impregnated by His holy presence. Everything that touches us calls us to God. The mind plunges into the inner, intimate depths of things and finds God always as the immanent principle that sustains all creatures in being.

No longer is there a sacred and a secular world. Instead, one now moves, not as an angel by-passing or ignoring this world, but rather seeing the world in all its uniqueness, and yet seeing it in the finality of God's creative love. Such a person has entered into true freedom. No longer does such a person see only in the light of his own petty world or of his own desires, so inordinate at times, but now he has died to self and lives to Christ. Surely this is the dimension that Paul had experienced when he repeated these words in his epistles: to put on Christ, to live in Christ, to be with Christ. One hundred and sixty-four times Paul uses this phrase, "in Christ." When we move through the purification of self, we open ourselves totally to God's presence, and we begin to see Christ in all things and all things in Christ.

You start with a stone, a little flower—God is there, totally. One does not have to run over the whole world and to exhaust the gamut of human experiences in order to find God. In the beginning, contemplative souls need beautiful trees and flowers. As they become more and more advanced in contemplation, they follow the instruction of Evagrius, desert Father of the fourth century: "Go into your cell—go into your cell and don't come out. It will teach you everything." If you have God, you have everything, because you are touching the core of reality.

In this stage of prayer, there is a great experience of unity in finding God in all things. The dichotomy between action and contemplation does not exist any more. Whatever the person is doing—opening or closing his eyes, he finds the Divine Presence everywhere in the unity of all things, and this forces the person out of himself in a spirit of worship and service.

This, it seems to me, is the only real celibate. This is celibacy ultimately, not so much physically, but theologically—the celibacy of one who is now totally open to the presence of God and in love with the whole world, because the person has already participated in an experience similar to the Beatific Vision of God in all things and all things in God. This person of prayer cannot for a moment love another human being for himself alone. Yet he does not love another person only as a *means* to God. The process is more intuitive, and this he cannot explain. It is an experience of God at the heart of all matter. He loves this being, this person, this tree, this stone, and God at the same time. There is no moving from this to that, but in his vision he sees at one and the same time the created being and the infinite love of God Who creates this being and gives it to him as a gift. He finds the gift and Giver in the same look.

The actual graces in which God manifests Himself are very numerous and variable for each contemplative. There are likes, tastes, intuitions, attractions that draw the soul to an understanding of God working in all types, in all manners of persons and events. In one moment, suddenly the person realizes that God is there, that God exists—"My God! He loves me!"—a tremendous grace, a breakthrough in consciousness. But normally, besides these great moments of illumination that follow upon this new plateau of "seeing" God in all things, day after day, moment after moment there is a continued evolution of the soul in an imperceptible presence of God in solitude that leads to even greater and greater unity. There are great moments that come like flashes, but normally there is a steady growth that leads to a higher degree still to come, the step that makes the soul die to itself in a complete love of others.

"LOVE ONE ANOTHER AS I HAVE LOVED YOU"

This degree ultimately is where the vision of unity is leading us. The more one is raised to the intimate presence of God, the experience of the knowledge and love of God, the more he begins to enter into communion with other human beings. There develops within us a genuine sense of being one with the whole world, of being open and ready to give ourselves to the world and more specifically to the community in which we find ourselves.

It would be very superficial to think that a person, having found God, would then turn to the world in the sense of mere pity or condescending compassion. On the contrary, in discovering God he discovers the most intimate bond of all creation, and so in his relationship to God he moves out into a community where God is found as the creative force. That person is he who makes the synthesis between the first and second commandments and finds that there are not two commandments but really only one: we must love the Lord our God with our whole mind and our whole soul. The love of God cannot kill our love for other human beings. True love of God will always be a true love for other human beings. There is only one love.

> Let us love one another since love comes from God
> And everyone who loves is begotten by God
>   and knows God.
> Anyone who fails to love can never have known God.
> —as long as we love one another God will live in us
> And his love will be complete in us. . .
> God is love and anyone who lives in love
>   lives in God,
> And God lives in him (I Jn. 4;7-16).

If we, then, by experiencing this love of God within us, yield to this love, it is the nature of God's love to communicate itself to others. Thus the very community of the Trinity loving within us pushes outside of us and through us to bring about, in the immediate world around us, a similar Trinitarian community of Godly loving persons. It happens often, when a soul is drawn to God in this period of greater silence and solitude, that there is a period when a person cannot go out, cannot feel this warm rapport with others. One's interior is so totally fixed upon God that such a person feels "out of it"; human commerce seems useless and banal. That is, I suppose, one of the trials of the spiritual life, this sense of impotence to witness sufficiently to the love of God that we have experienced so abundantly within us. Here we must keep in mind the need to be humble and open to serve all who come into our little world, even though we should bungle and not succeed in doing much.

God does give an attraction to a deep contemplative life that often means a forced cutting off of oneself from the usual contacts with other human beings beyond the immediate and closed circle of members of a chosen religious community. Such a person is called to witness to that eschatological total immersion in God that will be our life to come. But this does not mean that such a contemplative can be indifferent to the world. Evagrius of the desert said: "I leave men in order to find them." In our pragmatic life, ruled by worldly standards, this type of life, to be totally absorbed in God, to be at the total disposition of God, asking to do only what He wants and never seeking self, seems absurd and impractical. The world needs this type of absurdity and impracticality. Such absurdity will make sense only in the life to come or to persons of faith who can appreciate the value of such prophetic signs.

If one thinks being a contemplative in such a hidden life is egotistic and easy, then he has not lived such a life to its fullest. We read in the lives of the early Fathers of the desert, about those who anticipated the cosmic redemption of the world by entering deeply into themselves; in their hidden life they became re-concilers with Christ in order to effect the redemption of one particle of this universe and thus in some small way extend that redemption into the world without ever going out into the world. But most of us God is not calling to this absolute immediacy as a sign to the world of the *eschaton* to come. But He is calling all of us to be contemplatives in this sense: to love the Lord our God with our whole heart, our whole soul, our whole mind, our whole strength—this is to be a contemplative, to look at God as the root of our being and to love Him in all things.

God calls us to love, and now on earth as later in heaven, we are to spend our eternity growing in the love of God as mirrored in other beings. Heaven is going to be this whole wonderful world transfigured by the presence of God through an ever-increasing degree of consciousness of His presence and love. We can test whether God has really brought us to a true experience in contemplation of the indwelling Trinity, by our ability to go out and love others as God has loved us. The contemplative sees himself as a person loved by God very much, and in this grace he discovers himself more centered upon God, more one with God, and yet more one with all other beings. There is no longer fear or a sense of insecurity. He is rooted in God and he can go forth and love the world as God loves it. So the presence of God in all things evolves into an habitual experience that allows the contemplative to move always from light to light, "from glory to glory." Every day is a new romance of discovery.

This is contemplation. It is not just turning aside to be alone with God for an hour. It is the gift of God's loving presence within us so strongly felt that we can find God everywhere and praise Him in union with all the living and the dead. We realize that the dead who passed beyond this worldly existence are really not dead but are more alive than we. We learn to communicate with them, for they see reality in its fullness. By our faith we can join them and praise God continually. This is what a contemplative is, and it seems to me that it is also a very good description of what it means to be a human being.

3

The Eastern Heritage of Christian Mysticism

LUX EX ORIENTE

We have already mentioned the recent openness of Westerners to insights and practices coming from Far Eastern religions. What can a Western man, especially a Christian, learn from such practices? I would like to offer some suggestions towards a Christian Yoga that would offer help to a deeper mysticism for Westerners, and would show the influence of Far Eastern mysticism on that of the Christian East. Then we can move into the insights and practices for mysticism that have come to us from the Eastern Christian world, certainly influenced through Moslem and Hindu mysticism in its evolution towards what we know as Byzantine spirituality.

What is the chief attraction in the Eastern religions? Western man is more and more turning toward them for a different approach to Reality. Descartes' "clear and distinct ideas" have given the West a rationalistic science of theology. Yet man hungers desperately for an immediate encounter with the God of Abraham, Isaac and Jacob. When Western man prays, he does so with his head. He is a performer, a doer, an actor. He is busy; he has lost the art of being still and of listening to God speaking in the depths of his being. The Semitic or Eastern approach is instead one of the heart. Man descends into his inner self and there listens to the transcendent God who is "closer to us than our most inward part and higher than our highest," as St. Augustine confesses.

Western man will eventually create his own type of Yoga in order to expand his consciousness. However, it is my believe from personal experience that the various aspects of Yoga coming from the East (including the Eastern Christian Byzantine style) can be of great help to all serious-minded persons eager to advance in contemplation.

The first area of profit is to share in the integration of body, soul, and spirit that is one of the preliminary aims of any Yogic exercise. The Western dichotomy that pits matter against spirit, body against soul, makes it next to impossible for man to become integrated. Our competitive society, dominated by puritanical notions of good and evil and by the compulsion always to act according to the preconceived self-image imposed by society, does not allow us to be quiet and, like children, to sense deeply the present moment and the real self made aware of itself by profound sense impressions of the immediate world around it. Instead of being compelled to *do,* we must learn just to *be* in a living, dynamic flow of energy all around us, open and receptive to its creative power.

YOGIC CONCENTRATION

Thousands of years before the advent of Christianity, Hindu sannyasa hit upon the lotus position as one giving maximum relaxation and integration of body and spirit. Whatever position one assumes (it is often dependent upon physical training over a long period), one should be relaxed and comfortable but wide awake. Krishna advises Arjuna in the *Baghadvad Gita:* "Being seated there, making the mind one-pointed and subduing activities of mind and senses, let him practice Yoga for self-purification."

A way of becoming "one-pointed," suggested by Yoga, is to look intently upon a flower, a painting, or some object of beauty. Focus upon it with all your senses. Try to devour it with your eyes. Listen to the music of its colors. Smell its special fragrant beauty. Become immersed into the object so that soon the distance between you and the object is overcome, and you feel one with the object contemplated. Gradually, a feeling that admits of great intensity and growth allows you to transcend the tyranny of your "conditioned" self and the limitations of place, time, and uncontrolled desires.

Through such disciplined concentration you will not only begin to perceive a oneness with the world outside you but also a slowing down of your mental activities with an accompanying sense of deep peace and quiet.

This is a sign of an integration process taking place, where the mind, as the Byzantine Hesychasts of Mount Athos described it, is forced into the "heart," the deepest level of man's existence where he experiences himself immersed in God who is the core or ground of his being.

THE JESUS PRAYER

Another Yogic form of concentration is the use of a *mantra.* By focusing the senses and imagination upon a word or phrase such as "Rama, Rama" or "Namah Shivaya," the Hindu contemplative is able to descend into his *Guha,* the cave of his heart, and there take the great leap where he can pass to the other bank of his true self. The Byzantine Christian world, inheriting a Jesus-centered spirituality from Macarius and the early Fathers of the Egyptian desert, combined the recitation of the Jesus Prayer with one's breathing: "Lord, Jesus Christ, Son of God, have mercy on me, a sinner." St. John Climacus in his *Ladder of Perfection* exhorts Christians: "May the memory of Jesus combine with your breathing; then you will understand the use of silence."

This simple prayer, much like the Hail Mary forming the Rosary in the West, was first repeated reverently with the lips, then in the mind with greater concentration on the presence of the risen Lord within the contemplative. Finally the Name of Jesus became centered in the heart, became fused with the total person praying. The senses, emotions, imagination, intellect, and will all converged upon the presence of the Lord.

SILENT LISTENING

We realize that any such techniques do not constitute contemplation, at least as the word is used in the Christian sense. But they can powerfully help a contemplative to withdraw from the disharmonious world of multiplicity in order to "recollect" himself, to pull himself to his center and there in humble adoration yield to the Speech of God.

Yoga offers physiological and psychological aids to prepare for the contemplation that, in the tranquility of all one's faculties, first appears as a listening to God in quietness and silence.

Through such total, ontological listening man allows the hidden powers in himself to come forth. The total person begins to realize God's presence permeating his whole being. Man begins to experience God not through knowledge where the mind looks at God through the medium of a mental picture but through God's pervading presence as light. The Upanishads describe His presence as: "He is down there, He is here, quite close. He is within all that is; from all that is. He is apart. He is everywhere shining, bodiless without limbs, seeing, wise, born of Himself. He it is who orders everything aright throughout the eternal years."

Meister Eckhart, the 14th century Rhineland mystic, speaks of the experience common to all mystics when they have entered deeply into the "cave of the heart": "It may be asked whether this birth is best accomplished in man when he does the work and forms and thinks himself into God, or when he keeps himself in silence, stillness, and peace, so that God may speak and work in him. . .the best and noblest way in which you may come into this work and life is by keeping silence and letting God work and speak. When all the powers are withdrawn from their work and images, there is this word spoken."

NON-DUALITY OF GOD

One of the important contributions of Eastern Yogic meditation for contemplatives in the West is to offer a corrective against the subject-object separation of the contemplative and God. For the Eastern mind contemplating God in the depths of his being, the emphasis is on the plenitude or fullness of God and His all-pervading presence. The Isha Upanishad proclaims the All-in-Allness of God within man so that there remains nowhere inside man where God is not: "Plenitude everywhere; Plenitude there, here. From Plenitude comes forth Plenitude and everywhere one with itself there remains Plenitude."

For the Western mind good is opposed to bad, birth to death, finity to infinity. But to oppose God as infinite to everything as finite is to set up a false duality. God's plenitude cannot be placed within an oppositional duality.

The Hindu *Advaita* or non-duality is a theological statement that flows out of an in-depth experience of God as the ocean of being in which man floats as a drop. It preserves the mystery that cannot be unraveled through an intellectual process but which can be approached only in the darkness of paradoxes. The Upanishad literature expresses this mystery: "He is not known by him who knows Him, not understood by him who understands. He alone contemplates Him who has ceased to contemplate Him. In all knowledge as though by intuition, the wise man finds Him. It is in Him alone, the Atman, that each one is strong. It is in knowing Him alone that one becomes immortal. A great loss it is, in truth, for him who does not attain Him here below."

For the Eastern contemplative to explain the union of God and man by any limiting concepts is to deflower the real experience. And yet any contemplative, from either the East or the West, knows from experience, once he has entered into the interior castle, that God is never an object to be looked at and petitioned. God is experienced as present to the contemplative as breath is in the breather.

JOURNEY TOWARDS CENTER

Any true contemplative, deeply encountering God, realizes in an unending process of education, the work chiefly of Divine Wisdom, that it is God who reveals Himself as always present. The "journey towards center" becomes gradually an experienced pull on God's part and less man's effort to attain. Yet man can learn to pull himself together, he can be taught how to pass through the various outer chambers. Once each person is within his center, only the Holy Spirit can lead him, since the assimilation of man into God's own life is done only in an experience of God's perfect love and · man's complete nothingness.

Eastern religions, especially their Yogic techniques for breaking down the barriers between our "outer" surface self and our deeper, "truer" self, can help the Western mind to prepare itself for the higher reaches of infused contemplation. Contemplation is a continued process, a growth in total immersion in God through grace. A Christian Yoga can prepare us for the expansion of consciousness by teaching us how to move beyond the duality of discursive prayer into an imageless experience of God as the burning Source of love begetting His Son in an act of complete self-giving and the Son in His Spirit of Love surrendering Himself in complete service back to the Father.

EASTERN CHRISTIAN MYSTICISM

Christianity was born as the flowering of Judaism. Moses was the model of Semite mysticism: one who in awe and trembling dared not to look upon the face of Yahweh but rather listened to the Word of God. Moses met God on top of Mount Sinai in the cloud of darkness amidst thundering and lightening. The accent is on the existential encounter with the Absolute, not in images, concepts or through a reasoning process, but through a reverent, silent listening.

As St. John's Gospel portrays the incarnate Word of God, God is life, to be experienced, received, to be the new force to make us into children of God. Christ is the Life of God and is our true, full life. The early Christian documents, therefore, transmit faith, the Gospel and the sacraments under the aspect of life. Faith is the germ of life. To preach the Gospel is to sow the word of life. This new life is given in Baptism. In the immersion of the Christian into the waters of Baptism, the total man is submerged in death to selfish sinning in order that the same total man may put on the new life brought to us through Christ. Salvation is a new life in Christ that has to grow and possess our consciousness more and more.

Gradually there appeared in Christianity a shift from the existential approach to a more intellectual approach. Origen developed the Platonic concept of life assimilating light. Evagrius of Pontus, who has been described as a Christian Buddhist, defined prayer in terms of the mind: "The state of prayer is a passionless state in which supreme love transports on high a wisdom-loving spiritual mind."[1]

God was now to be seen by the intellect of man turned within. We see the basis now for a hesychasm that would soon develop around this inner light. God is now experienced as light in an intellectual vision. This is the doctrine of the Alexandrian School, developed largely in the mysticism of Clement of Alexandria, Origen, and Evagrius of Pontus.

The more Semitic influence, with its accent on the total, existential encounter with God in the "heart," continued chiefly in the Antiochene School of Ignatius of Antioch, Polycarp, Irenaeus, Macarius and Antony of the desert and the whole school of mystics that placed the accent on an affective encounter in the "heart" with Jesus as Lord. It is the heart, not the mind, where God is encountered as the source of life. The Jesus Prayer would develop from the affective heart-spirituality more so than from a spirituality of intellectualism. By reverently pronouncing the name of Jesus, the Christian mystic in the desert was immersed in the presence of the Risen Lord. Here we encounter an existential spirituality built around a mysticism of darkness, not light. It is temerity to approach God by any human reasoning; it is by purification of the heart that man disposes himself, and then God reveals Himself as the Life-giver not by means of any intellectual experience but in the darkening of man's intellect. It is this "apophatic" spirituality that I would like to develop, for it has a certain resonance common to the Far Eastern mysticism and a definitely needed emphasis for modern Christian mysticism.

APOPHATIC SPIRITUALITY

Perhaps the distinguishing characteristic of Eastern Christian mysticism is its apophatic quality. Similar to Far Eastern mysticism, Eastern Christian mysticism insists that the highest union, the infused union where God speaks to us directly about Himself, is not achieved in any conceptual knowledge but in an immediate, experimental knowledge wherein He opens Himself to us. We can never come to this knowledge through any concept, through any rationalization or any discursive method of our own. God, purely and simply and in His Transcendence, reveals Himself to us when He wishes. After years of our own preparation and cooperation through continued purification, God sees that we are humble enough to be so open to Him as to see Him in everything and to see ourselves as an off-shoot of God's overflowing love.

Thus, the Eastern Fathers developed the highest type of contemplation in terms of an apophatic theology. Apophatic is usually translated as negative, but this is to misunderstand the nuanced mysticism of these early Fathers. The accent is entirely on God doing the revealing, giving the Gift of Himself; no longer with the emphasis on man and his personal activity. God who is so infinitely perfect and good, the incomprehensible, deigns to allow us to know Him in some fashion or other by way of a direct experience.

The other manner of knowing God, cataphatic or positive assertion about God's attributes, is used by the Eastern Fathers but more or less as a preparation for the higher stages of contemplation. The cataphatic theology uses the perfections that we find in creatures about us, and from this limited knowledge we are able to know something about the infinite perfections of God. The apophatic approach, coming as a preparation for a higher, more unitive experience of God, tells us constantly: "But it is never really this way at all." We move from a beginning stage of positive concept of God to a higher stage. This latter is, as Pseudo-Dionysius says, "In darkness that you see." It is a paradox that in utter darkness God reveals Himself. We remove ourselves from any possibility of coming to know God by our own power, and in that utter state of humility and nothingness and abasement before God, witnessing to that ontological truth that we are creatures dependent on God, He then comes down and shows Himself to us in that darkness or incapacity of our own natural faculties.

Apophatic theology is far from being purely negative. Purification or catharsis is necessary to effect the gradual ascent to God, like Moses going to Mount Sinai. Nikos

Kazantzakis has described this struggle to yield to God: "God is fire, and you must walk on it. . .dance on it. At that moment the fire will become cool water. But until you reach that point, what a struggle, my Lord, what agony!"

Along the way, God demands that we separate ourselves from the things of this world until we reach the very top of the mountain, and then in the darkness of the storming clouds we hear the notes of the trumpet and we see those lights that no human method could ever give us. This is one reason why, if we read the Fathers of the desert, we will never find a discursive treatise on prayer. It is just impossible to "methodize" the most intimate stages of assimilation by loving surrender into God. These Fathers could give to a disciple "a word by which they could be saved," a word that could prepare the groundwork. They could tell a disciple how to fast and make vigils, do penance, cry out for tears and a continued state of compunction, and how to say the Jesus Prayer, but ultimately they knew that God had to take over eventually, and then it was a matter of personal experience. No one but God could give that experience.

St. John Damascene describes this approach:

> God is infinite and incomprehensible and all that is comprehensible about Him is His infinity and incomprehensibility. All that we can say cataphatically concerning God does not show forth His nature, but things that relate to His nature. God does not belong to a class of existing things. He receives no existence, but is above all existing things. If all forms of knowledge have to do with what exists, that which is above knowledge must be above all (created) essence, and what is above essence must be above knowledge.[2]

ST. GREGORY OF NYSSA'S MYSTICISM OF DARKNESS

Gregory of Nyssa, along with his master, Origen, is one of the most original thinkers of the Eastern Church and the one who perhaps had the greatest influence in Christian mysticism. Pseudo-Dionysius in his mystical theology treatise is directly dependent upon Gregory. Through Pseudo-Dionysius this mysticism of darkness reached the West mainly through the Rhenish mystics of the 14th century: Meister Eckhart, Tauler and Suso, and the Flemish mystic, Jan Ruysbroeck, all of whom had at least an indirect influence upon Spanish mysticism of the 16th century, chiefly upon St. John of the Cross and St. Teresa of Avila.

The theology of darkness is not original with Gregory but is basically derived from Philo (+44), the Alexandrian Hellenistic Jew. Both Gregory and Philo saw the mystical connotations of the Exodus theme as an analogy of the journey of the individual toward full union with God. Is is especially in Gregory's treatise on the *Life of Moses* that we have a full presentation of the soul's journey up the mountain to meet God in the darkness of unknowing. In this work Gregory develops the meaning of darkness. Although it does mean, as has been already stated, that man possesses an incapacity to know God intimately, it primarily means that God is absolutely unfathomable, the fullness of being, and man can "understand" this only in darkness.

Like Moses' ascent of Mount Sinai, the movement of the individual soul towards enlightenment begins in darkness of sin. He sees a ray of the light of God that beckons him to leave the foothills and start climbing upward. The higher stages are degrees of his entrance into the darkness of God's incomprehensibility. Gregory states this in his *Commentary on the Song of Songs:*

> Our initial withdrawal from wrong and erroneous ideas of God is a transition from darkness to light. Next comes a closer awareness of hidden things, and by this the soul is guided through sense phenomena to the world of the invisible. And this awareness is a kind of cloud, which overshadows all appearances, and slowly guides and accustoms the soul to look towards what is hidden. Next the soul makes progress through all these stages and goes on higher, and as she leaves behind all that human nature can attain, she enters within the secret chamber of the divine knowledge, and here she is cut off on all sides by the divine darkness. Now she leaves outside all that can be grasped by sense or by reason, and the only thing left for her contemplation is the invisible and the incomprehensible.[3]

It should be noted that for Gregory the movement is not from darkness to light solely, but it is a continual process from darkness to light and then to darkness and again to light.[4]

THE TRANSCENDENCE OF GOD

In his apophatic approach, Gregory is too much absorbed in the awesome transcendence of God to be preoccupied with man's incapacity. He takes time out only to stress that all representation of God is for the mystic an obstacle to God's further revelation once a stage of entering "into the cloud" has begun. True knowledge of God is not to be found where man searches for it.[5]

V. Lossky describes this knowledge of God beyond all conceptualization:

> .. .having failed to recognize the One it desires among the intelligible and incorporal beings, and abandoning all that it

finds, it recognized the One it is seeking as the only One he does not comprehend. . .Union with God is presented as a path which goes beyond vision, intelligence to the area where knowledge is suppressed and love alone remains—or rather where gnosis becomes agape.[6]

One must note that the overwhelming infinity of God is nevertheless an experienced presence of God to the contemplative. But the modality of recognizing this presence is a new and higher form of knowledge that surpasses the powers and experiences of man. Thus Gregory resorts to such paradoxical terms as "luminous darkness," "sober inebriation," etc. Gregory describes this presence without seeing in his *Commentary on the Song of Songs:*

> The Bride is surrounded with the divine night in which
> the Bridegroom comes near without showing Himself. . .
> but by giving the soul a certain sense of His presence
> while fleeing from clear knowledge.[7]

The presence and the transcendence of God are one in Gregory's apophatic mysticism. It is only because God is so supremely transcendent that He can be present to man as intimately as though He were man's very being, which He is. The closer one approaches to union with God, the more blinding God appears. It is not a question of the knowledge of God becoming more abstruse but of the nature of God becoming more present. This presence makes man realize the absolute awesomeness of what the end of his journey will be like.

THE LIFE OF MOSES

It is in his classical treatise on the life of Moses that Gregory best expounds his particular teaching on apophatic mysticism. With Philo, he sees that the journey of Israel from Egypt to the Promised Land corresponds to the progress of the individual soul in its march towards the perfection of contemplation. Gregory expounds his understanding of the mystical life in commenting on the long journey. He stresses the necessity of purification from vice and sensuousness by means of the stories of Moses and the plagues and the idolatry of the Isrealites in the desert. The sacrament of Baptism is seen in the crossing of the Red Sea. The Bread from Heaven is now the soul's contemplation of the Transcendent One.

In a rather long citation that is essential to the understanding of Gregory's doctrine, he states:

> But what now is the meaning of Moses' entry into the darkness and of the vision of God that he enjoyed in it? The present text (Exod. 24, 15) would seem to be somewhat contradictory to the divine apparition he has seen before. There he saw God in the light (burning bush), whereas here he sees Him in the darkness. But we should not therefore think that this contradicts the entire sequence of spiritual lessons which we have been considering. For the sacred text is here teaching us that spiritual knowledge first occurs as an illumination in those who experience it. Indeed, all that is opposed to piety is conceived of as darkness; to shun the darkness is to share in the light. But as the soul makes progress, and by a greater and more perfect concentration comes to appreciate what knowledge of truth is, the more it approaches this vision, and so much the more does it see that the divine nature is invisible.
>
> It thus leaves all surface appearances, not only those that can be grasped by the senses, but also those which the mind itself seems to see, and it keeps on going deeper until by the operation of the Spirit it penetrates the invisible and incomprehensible, and it is there that it sees God. The true vision and the true knowledge of what we seek consists precisely in not seeing, in an awareness that our goal transcends all knowledge and is everywhere cut off from us by the darkness of incomprehensibility. Thus that profound Evangelist, John,

who penetrated into this luminous darkness, tells us that no man has seen God at any time (Jn. 1,18), teaching us by this negation that no man—indeed, no created intellect—can attain a knowledge of God.[8]

We have moved far into intimate knowledge of God, into a vision that sees nothing, a darkness that enlightens, a transcendence of God that brings Him immanently present to the contemplative.

EPECTASIS: LOVE, NEVER STATIC, ALWAYS GROWING

Gregory, who sought to rectify the teachings of Origen on the pre-existence of souls, nevertheless seized upon the truly positive insights of Origen and developed them further. A key insight taken from Origen is that the love of God in man is a force expanding his being and making him infinitely capable of possessing God in an unending process of greater growth. Gregory describes true perfection as "never to stop growing towards what is better and never to place any limit on perfection."[9]

Grace or the life of God within man, both in this life and in the life to come, presupposes growth in accepting a loving relationship with God and implies the necessity of constantly moving toward God. Gregory writes: "Seeing that it is of the nature of Goodness to attract those who raise their eyes towards it, the soul keeps rising ever higher and higher." [10]

Gregory gives us two reasons, still viable for us today, why man's progress toward God can never come to an end. The first reason is that Beauty, God Himself, is infinite. The second reason is that the Beautiful is of such a nature that the desire for it can never be fully

persons and corporately in society, of all the demonic forces that bind us to a darkening, crippling slavery. We wish to be freed of our sinful past, to grow unceasingly into fuller health and happiness.

If we as Christians have progressed somewhat in the awareness of God's breath that He continually breathes into us His Spirit of love, we know that only the power of Jesus Christ can heal and free us to be what we should be by our first creation. Only He is the external Image of God the Father. We have been begotten in His Spirit to be sons of God and co-heirs with Him of Heaven forever.

Mysticism (prescinding from erroneous manifestations of a basic human drive for union with the Absolute Transcendent) is the movement of a humble soul on fire with love for God towards greater union. In the growing assimilation into God's very life lies our consciousness of uniqueness. The mystic that has experienced the personal love of God and is conscious that God accepts him, loves him, suffers for him even to the point of accepting death on the Cross, can alone love others as man should love. The mystic realizes that he has become fire and light. God, infinite love, loves within him. His wisdom is to be one with Him. This is love experienced that begets love towards others. True mysticism is authenticated by the love that the mystic shows towards others in humble service, for this alone, the acceptance of others in self-sacrificing love, proves that the mystic has experienced a true love from the Source of all beauty and goodness. Mysticism that does not reap a harvest in shared love towards others is a deception and in the end is dehumanizing. True mysticism is always begetting, becoming the other in greater unity of love. On this point, Eastern Christian mysticism has much to teach us.

4

The Jesus Prayer

We see taking place, throughout the whole Church and throughout all society, what Teilhard de Chardin called the process of convergence and of hominization, the process whereby the human race is consciously growing into a "global village." Man is his brother's keeper, wherever in this whole universe he may be found. The media of communication have given us the possibility of knowing that my brother is in Bangladesh because I have literally *seen* him suffer. In our very recent past we have seen men walking on the moon, and suddenly planetary distances do not exist as they did before. In a moment I can be present in a psychic way to the needs of everyone throughout the world.

Hence in the thrust towards a new and greater awareness of the value of each human person, we see that we must move toward a greater in-depth personal prayer. We can likewise see the basis for the movement, as has been pointed out earlier, toward becoming integrated in body, soul, and Spirit, and toward using Yoga, Zen, proper breathing techniques, the emptying of the mind through a process of relaxation, etc. as "standard equipment" for the contemplative today.

This new understanding of the human person can also explain the recent discovery of the Jesus Prayer by those seriously seeking a more personal contact with the Lord. The *Philokalia* has preserved for us the tradition of the monks of the desert, who did not only repeat the Jesus Prayer: "Lord, Jesus Christ, Son of God, have mercy on me, a sinner," merely as one prays this or that ejaculation. To these simple "children of the kingdom of Heaven," the Spirit revealed the essence of the Jesus-event in a living experience. These were indeed "Jesus people," the true "Jesus freaks" whose love for Him was more durable than a mere fad.

These were the charismatics of the early period of Christianity who, when baptized in the Holy Spirit, experienced, as we still do today, a vivid realization of the power in the name of Jesus. It is the Spirit of Jesus that reveals to us all we need to know of Jesus as our Lord and Savior. ". . .The Holy Spirit, whom the Father will send in my *name*, will be your teacher and will bring to your minds all that I have said to you" (Jn. 14, 26).

These athletes of Christ knew from their experience in the desert that there is no other name whereby we are to be saved. Like Peter after curing the cripple before the Gate Beautiful of the Temple, we too must profess loudly to the whole world: "It is the *Name* of this same Jesus; it is faith in that *Name*, which has cured this man. . ." (Acts 3, 16).

They witnessed with Paul to the sacred power of that Name. "God has given Him a name that is above all names so that at the name of Jesus every knee shall bend in heaven, on earth, and under the earth" (Phil. 2:9-10).

KNOWLEDGE OF THE HEART

Carl Jung has shown great interest in the approach to reality through the "heart." In a study of the American Pueblo Indians, he found that the Indian rejected the white man's rational type of knowledge in favor of his own type of "thinking in the heart." The so-called Hellenistic approach to reality is one of abstraction to arrive at an essential knowledge; the essence conceived in a clear and distinct idea is important; the individual is of no concern. In contrast to this approach, the Old and New Testaments reveal to us a childlike openness to reality, a way of approaching the whole of reality and letting it be as it is, without the "will to power" attempting to change and convert it into something new according to man's own conceptualization.

Most early, unsophisticated societies approached reality in such a total experience. They knew nothing of the Western dichotomy between body and soul, matter and spirit. Man was a part of the material world, and he entered into true knowledge, total experience of it through healthy sense impressions. This seems to be at the basis of St. Benedict's spirituality, which encouraged contact with the material world surrounding the monk through vivid sense experiences, so that he might, in a sense of self-identity through interaction with the creation, live in God's real, existential world and thus pray always.

To love is the work of the mystic, and love cannot be conceptualized; it can only be experienced. Our Western mind is full of ideas, abstractions. We are always chattering noisily about an abstract world, while the real world recedes farther and farther from us. In all our activity, we are driven by a spirit of competition. We are conditioned to have a fixed self-image that remains intact even while we submit to constant pressures to be something in particular. Hence when we try to quiet the mind by concentrating on being one with the immediate world around us, we find ourselves beseiged by thoughts and desires. Our true self is imprisoned by the false ego that is culturally hypnotized in the direction of endless conditional commandments.

We have lost the wonderment of children who can enjoy simple reality with a curiosity and openness that allows them to *be there,* rather than wanting always to *do* something. Is it any wonder that if we were to stop and relax for a moment, we would soon realize how bound up we are; how our breathing is not allowed to proceed freely; and how we are not free to be our true selves.

We live in the mind and disregard the body. We have forgotten the simple rhythm that God has planted within all of us: the rhythm of our breath, which allows us to descend beyond our habitual self-hypnosis to enter into an inner world of freedom where the Transcendent God becomes the Immanent Ground of our being.

MANTRA

In all religions we find the ancient practice of either continuously chanting or reciting aloud or mentally repeating a set phrase. In the Hindu tradition, this practice involves the chanting of the *Om Shanti* or some other mantra given the disciple by the guru; in the Zen Buddhist tradition, it might be a *koan* which, repeated at least mentally, leads the disciple beyond conceptualization into the inner mystery of reality. In the Moslem tradition, it is the *dikhr* or Holy Name of Allah which, repeated continuously, renders Him present to the one in prayer.

In the Byzantine Christian East, the Christian learned to synchronize his breathing with the invocation of the sacred name of Jesus. With no discursive thought about the content of the prayer, the Byzantine Christian learned to occupy his senses and imagination with a fixed point of attention that then freed his mind to be free, docile, supple to God operating in a non-verbal manner.

But for the Christian of the East, the name itself was not unimportant. Christianity had sprung from the Semitic, biblical world based largely on an oral culture that placed much more importance on the spoken word than we do. For the ancients of the Bible, the spoken word revealed the personality and the intimate beliefs of the speaker. By understanding this background, especially the psychology of the Semite who believed the person named to be present to the one pronouncing the name with reverence and love, we can better appreciate not only the Christians' reverence and love for the name of Jesus, but also their insight into the presence of the Risen Savior by pronouncing that name. This understanding could open to us today a great source of biblical spirituality and a form of simple, relaxed prayer that could be most helpful for all of us in our everyday, dash-about world.

NEW TESTAMENT PIETY

The Jesus Prayer has its roots not only in the New Testament but even farther back in the Old Testament. In the Old Covenant we see a developed personal conviction that the invocation of the name of God brought with it the conscious realization of His Presence. "Call on my Name, I will hear" (Zec. 13, 9). Once a year on the day of Atonement, Yahweh's name was pronounced only by the high priest who was chosen to offer sacrifice inside the "Holy of Holies" of the temple in Jerusalem.

The New Testament gives us a fuller theology of God's name and the power that emanates from the reverent pronouncing of the name of Jesus. Philippians 2:9-10 tells us that "God has given Him a name that is above all names so that at the name of Jesus every knee shall bend in heaven, on earth and under the earth."

The Acts of the Apostles describe how the good news is preached in the name of Jesus. Converts believe Jesus is truly the Son of God; Christians encounter Him in the sacraments which are administered in His sacred name; miracles are wrought by uttering His name; martyrs die, pronouncing it reverently.

There is no tone of magic; only a deep conviction among the early Christians that Jesus Christ, true God and true man, who died and was raised up by His heavenly Father, still lived within them and was leading them to a share in His resurrected life. The Gospel stories of the two blind men on the road crying, "Son of David, have mercy on us" (Mt. 9, 27) and the humble request of the publican, "O God, have mercy on me, a sinner" (Lk. 18, 13) became the inspiration for this prayer.

THE PRAYER OF THE HEART

The early monks fled into the desert where, deprived of all but the barest necessities for maintaining life, they purified themselves from all attachments in order to listen to God in the clear, pure atmosphere of deep silence and solitude. With David the penitent, they could say: "I am worn out with groaning. Every night I drench my pillow and soak my bed with tears" (Ps. 6, 6).

Evagrius in his treatise on prayer exhorts Christians: "Before all else, pray to be given tears, that weeping may soften the savage hardness which is in your soul and, having acknowledged your sin unto the Lord (Ps. 31, 5), you may receive from Him the remission of sins." They desired to be penetrated with as deep a sorrow as possible before the goodness of God; the compunction or abiding sense of sorrow that they sought was the corrective to a distorted vision of reality centered in an illusory self-importance. Thus the early Fathers of the desert insisted on crying unceasingly to God for mercy. As an expression of this cry, Macarius of Egypt and his followers developed the monologue prayer; its essential element was a brief phrase repeating the name of God as Lord.

In the latter part of the fifth century, an unknown author, possibly Syrian, wrote the *Spiritual Homilies,* later attributed to St. Macarius. He develops a spirituality of the heart centered entirely on the Incarnate Word. Evagrian spirituality had equated man with a detached Platonic intellect. Disagreeing, Pseudo-Macarius shows us that the whole man, body and soul, must be re-integrated through rigorous asceticism and purification; he will then be able to control his thoughts by constantly living in the presence of God, and to become immersed in the divine life that lives within man.

In Macarius' 15th homily we read:

Even the Christian in this life can taste the grace of God which is the active power of the Spirit manifested in the heart of men. Sons of light, ministers of the New Covenant, they have nothing to learn near men. They learn by meeting God intimately. Grace itself inscribes on their hearts the laws of the Spirit. The heart is the master and king of all the corporal organs. Once grace seizes or takes over the grazing lands of the heart, it reigns over all members of man and over all his thoughts. It is there that she awaits the good. See why grace penetrates into all parts of the body.

Diadochus of Photike linked man's reintegration into the image and likeness of Jesus Christ with a constant remembrance of or living in the presence of Jesus Christ. St. John Climacus was perhaps the first to associate the "memory of Jesus" with man's breathing so as to make the presence of Christ a constant reality. In his *Ladder of Perfection* he exhorts Christians: "May the memory of Jesus combine with your breathing; then you will understand the use of silence."

Hesychius in his *Centuries* links the constant repetition of the name of Jesus to our breathing as the best means to keep ourselves open to God speaking within us. He writes:

> Blessed is he who cleaves with his thought to the prayer of Jesus, constantly calling to Him in his heart, just as air cleaves to our bodies or the flame to the candle. The sun, passing over the earth, produces daylight; and the holy and worshipful name of our Lord Jesus, constantly shining in the mind, produces a measureless number of sunlike thoughts.

A document accredited falsely to St. John Chrysostom formulated once and for all the Jesus Prayer in the form that we know it today. The attribution to John Chrysostom assured this text of the orthodoxy of its content and we can agree that it comes at the end of a long evolution which is of a consistent oneness. The text reads:

> I implore you, breathren, never to abandon the rule of prayer or neglect it. . .Eating and drinking, at home or on a journey, or whatever else he does, a monk should constantly call: 'Lord, Jesus Christ, Son of God, have mercy upon me.' This

remembering of the name of our Lord Jesus Christ should incite him to battle with the enemy. By this remembrance a soul forcing itself to this practice can discover everything which is within, both good and bad. First it will see within, in the heart, what is bad, and later—what is good. . .The name of our Lord Jesus Christ, descending into the depts of the heart will subdue the serpent holding sway over the pastures of the heart and will save our soul and bring it to life. Thus abide constantly with the name of our Lord Jesus Christ, so that the heart swallows the Lord and the Lord the heart and the two become one. But this work is not done in one or two days; it needs many years and a long time. For great and prolonged labor is needed to cast our the foe so that Christ dwells in us.

We see that these early Christians did not conceive the recitation of the Jesus Prayer as a mechanical device to induce a state of quietism where human effort ceased and sanctity was achieved as easily as breathing. The temptation to mechanize this meaningful prayer into a method can be attributed to a treatise called: *The Method of Hesychastic Prayer,* undoubtedly to be attributed to a certain Nicephoros. Here we see an influence on Byzantine spirituality from Muslim asceticism and ultimately from that of the Far East, especially Hindu Yoga and Zen Buddhism. Exact instructions are given on how to sit, suppressing one's breathing, gazing on one's navel, all the while trying to concentrate on entering into the so-called heart, the core of man's being.

In the 14th century St. Gregory of Sinai brought this method and the use of the Jesus Prayer to Mount Athos where a renaissance developed. This spirituality was carried to Russia and the other Slavic countries, especially through the publication in Slavonic and Russian of the *Philokalia,* the collection of writings of the leading Fathers of the hesychastic spirituality. Through the Orthodox and Eastern Catholics immigrating to the West, especially through the Russian and other Slav emigres, the Jesus Prayer has become known in Protestant and Catholic circles as well as among those of the Orthodox faith.

A modern man of the West might well ask whether this type of spirituality, centered around the constant repetition of the name of Jesus or (according to the traditional formula): "Lord, Jesus Christ, Son of God, have mercy on me, a sinner," has any meaning for him. Soren Kierkegaard sounded the alarm for modern man over a century ago, proclaiming the need for religious revolution. He warned: "Western civilization is approaching the end of an age and must either pass through a new religious mutation or lead to the total spiritual bankruptcy of Europe."

I think it can safely be said that we are beginning to feel something of this bankruptcy not only in Europe but here in America. The security that medieval Christianity felt within the confines of a highly structured, rationalistic theology has given way to a burning thirst for a more direct, interior experience of the transcendent Being.

Not only is the younger generation beginning to re-discover the beauty and the power of the name of Jesus, but they, and older Christians as well, are rejecting a jaded theology that has kept so many Christians from a living encounter with the Risen Lord.

The Jesus People proclaim the sweetness and lovableness of the name of Jesus. But we need to realize that, in our calling out to Jesus as Lord, there are three basic moments that a Christian must never forget. The Jesus freaks may be ignoring these.

A TRUE RELIGIOUS EXPERIENCE

Any true Christian religious experience must first of all place a strong accent on the awesomeness and complete *transcendence* of Jesus Christ. He is Lord! He is God! He is the Creator and Redeemer of us all. We must first recognize this terrifying fact. He is more than just a good man, more even than a Superstar! He is God! "Lord, Jesus Christ, Son of God!"

Secondly, we must recognize that we are sinners. St. James tells us to be humbled before God by realizing our sinfulness. "Realize that you have sinned and get your hands clean again. Realize that you have been disloyal and get your hearts made true once more. As you come close to God you should be deeply sorry, you should be grieved, you should even be in tears—you will have to feel very small in the sight of God before He will set you on your feet once more" (James 4: 7-10).

When we have lost a sense of our sinfulness, we have also lost our awareness of the constant need for a Savior.

"Lord Jesus Christ, have mercy on me a sinner!"

Thirdly, what binds us sinners to Jesus, the Lord and God Almighty, is that hunger to possess Jesus the Lord as immanently present within, "more intimate to me than I to myself." Because Jesus Christ is Lord and God, completely perfect and transcendent to all creatures, He is able also to be the ground of our being, living within us, sustaining us in being. "All creation took place through Him, and none took place without Him" (Jn. 1, 3). Paul tells us, "He is not far from anyone of us. Indeed, it is in Him that we live and move and have our being" (Acts 17, 28).

St. Peter typifies these three characteristics of a
religious experience. When Jesus told Peter and his
companions to lower their nets for a miraculous catch of
fish, Peter, overwhelmed by Jesus' power, threw himself at
His feet. "Depart from me, Lord, for I am a sinful man!"
(Lk. 5, 8). We can see his awe at the transcendence of
Jesus as the Son of God, accompanied by Peter's sense of
his own unworthiness before the greatness of the Lord,
and finally his desire to possess and hold Him, to cling to
His feet in adoring worship.

The Jesus Prayer is more than a prayer or ejaculation;
it is a way of life that should become as much a part of us
as our breathing. Said with conviction and lived in our
daily lives, this prayer confesses that He is Our "Lord Jesus
Christ, Son of God" and we humbly beg that He "have
mercy on us sinners."

Another aspect of the Jesus-Prayer spirituality that
we have great need of today is the sense of communal
sinfulness. This sense is developed as one repeats this
beautiful prayer. Would not the first step to genuine
intimacy with the Holy Trinity dwelling within us be, first
of all, an abiding compunction of heart, a state of sorrow,
both for corporate and personal sin? Carl Jung, the
psychologist of the collective unconscious, writes:

> Guilt, as a psychological phenomenon, involves every-
> body...A crime can never happen as our own consciousness
> sees it exclusively in and for itself. On the contrary, it happens
> in a wide radius. The wickedness of the others instantly
> becomes our own wickedness, because it kindles evil in our
> own soul. The crime has been partly suffered by everyone, and
> everyone has also partly committed it...No one need hope to
> escape this fact, for everybody harbors his 'statistical' criminal
> in himself...In order to be able at all to sever our union with
> evil, we really require a regular *rite de sortie:* a sort of

ceremony in which the judge, the hangman, and the people would solemnly declare their guilt and their willingness to make amends. If only men could see what personal enrichment comes out of recognizing their complicity in all that happens! What a sense of honesty and what a new spiritual honor that affords.

As we move to a greater creative union with all men to make this universe evolve into the fullness decreed by its Maker, and as we become more conscious of our dignity as co-creators with God in transfiguring this world into its maturity, we need a sense of corporate sorrow in order to attract the mercy of the Pantocrator towards the cosmos. The truths about God and man remain the same whether they are found in the Old Testament or the New, among the writings of the fiercely serious and practical Fathers of the desert or the more speculative Fathers of the Church; they are the same for Christians in the Middle Ages and for Christians in the 20th Century. Man will always remain the sinful creature obligated to cry out for mercy: "Amplius lava," "Lord, have mercy." And not only individual men, you and I, but the united human race needs a corporate sorrow. God will always remain the forgiving Lover, both of the individual sinner and of the sinful human race. Our abiding sorrow is that which alone brings us to true joy and ever new resurrection. Forgiveness overcomes fear and self-introspection and replaces it with the filial confidence of love: "Lord, have mercy on me, a sinner, on us sinners. Abba, Father."

Father Zossima in Dostoevsky's *Brothers Karamazov* expresses the secret of the transformation of this world: "To transform the world, to recreate it afresh, man must turn into another path psychologically. Until you have become, in actual fact, a brother to everyone, brotherhood will not come to pass. No sort of scientific teaching, no kind of common interest, will ever teach man to shore property and privilege with equal consideration for all."

In our urban, industrialized society, can we still encounter the living Savior? Can the reverential pronouncing of the sacred name of Jesus, preceded by our self-purification and our dying to all inordinate self-love, bring Him alive in our hearts and on our streets?

If we joined this prayer to a humble plea for the ability to see the all-ness of God in all things as we walk about our busy cities, drive along our highways, or occupy ourselves in an almost endless round of activities, would it not develop within us an atmosphere of God's presence that will enable us to see Him shining diaphanously in all His material creation?

By fidelity to such a simple, heartfelt encounter with the person Jesus through the repetition of His holy name, His presence will no longer be for us simply an object. We shall become more and more what God wants us to be in creating us to the image of His own divine Son. We shall become aware of our true self: not a subject adoring an object "far out there" or "above us" in the remoteness of heaven, but a child of God, a divinized being, participating, as St. Peter says, in the divine nature, without losing his own human nature. We shall not become God by nature, but nonetheless we shall truly be made God-like by His presence within. We shall come gradually to experience God deep down within our true person as the core of our very being. He who lives in the depths of our being will not be a mere concept but a living person, "closer to me than I am to myself," penetrating me completely.

A LESSON FROM THE EAST

We have much to learn from the spirituality of the early charismatic Eastern Christian Fathers that developed from a personal encounter with the person of Jesus Christ.

Pronouncing with deep reverence and faith the sacred *name* of Jesus, we bring His presence and power into our real life. The name of Jesus, pronounced with love, means that He is present as Lord, King, Sovereign Master. As we breathe in His *name* and power, we exhale our own sinfulness and that of the world around us. We call down the saving mercy of God upon a world that is "groaning in travail" (Rom. 8, 22).

APPLICATION TO OUR PERSONAL PRAYER-LIFE

There are various degrees of faith-appreciation of the presence of Jesus Christ in our lives. As we grow through life's desert experience into a deeper faith, our pronouncing of His holy Name will have ever greater effects on our prayer. At the beginning of our prayer-life, it can be used as an ejaculation throughout the day. It can also serve as a preparation for prayer, in order to integrate ourselves, to pull ourselves together and reach that "still point" deep within us where we know He lives and loves us.

Just as athletes and singers, speakers and performers on stage seek to bring themselves to the maximum degree of concentration and relaxation by deep, rhythmical breathing, so we can learn from them how to sit quietly and breathe properly. We follow the breath down deeply within us, trying to relax as the flow of energy courses through our being giving us new life and energy. When we feel that a basic rhythm of inhalation and exhalation has been established, we seek to synchronize our breathing with the reverent repetition of the Jesus Prayer. As we breathe in, we mentally say: "Lord, Jesus Christ." As we breathe out, we say: "Son of God." We breathe in again as we say: "Have mercy on me." And finally we breathe out with the words: "A sinner." Then the process is repeated.

If we are beginners in prayer, we can accompany such a recitation with simple reflections about the life of Jesus. If we have developed over years of mental prayer a deep awareness of the Lord's indwelling presence, we should not be concerned with ideas, images or any thought process.

We turn deeply within and find Jesus Christ within, sending His Spirit of love upon us. He it is who teaches us in a non-verbal way how to know the Father and His oneness with Jesus, the First-born of the Father. We are concerned with experiencing the salvific power of Jesus working upon our unredeemed selves. We do not seek a concept about Jesus as Savior, but we expose our sick selves to His healing power. Jesus in Hebrew means Savior. As we have said earlier, Savior means the *Healer,* the one who possesses full life and who can give us a share of this fullness. "And of His fullness we have all received" (Jn. 1, 16).

Only if we can experience, through the power of the revealing Spirit of Love, our illness and our inability to love in return for so much love received from God, can we possibly cry out to be healed. The same Spirit instills in us a confidence and childlike trust that the Father will give us what we ask in Jesus' sacred Name; "I tell you most solemnly, anything you ask for from the Father, He will grant in my name" (Jn 16:23-24). Jesus reveals to us the Father, and the Spirit instills within us the childlike confidence to believe that the Father truly will bestow the healing that we need. "...Ask and it will be given you; search and you will find, knock, and the door will be opened...What father among you would hand his son a stone when asked for bread? ...If you, then, who are evil, know how to give your children what is good, how much more will the heavenly Father give the Holy Spirit to those who ask Him!" (Lk. 11:9-13).

We begin gradually to experience what Peter preached in Acts, that there is no other Name whereby we are to be saved. If in a car accident we can cry out in our need to be saved: "Jesus Christ, help me!" we should continually in deep prayer be able also to cry out and then to experience the effect of such a heartfelt prayer. Jesus alone can bring us health. This Name that brings life should be on our lips day and night.

Pronouncing the Name of Jesus allows us to make His prayer our own and to enter into a greater sharing in His priesthood. This way of prayer is not a selfish "Jesus-and-I" piety. To the degree that we experience the tremendous love of God in Jesus Christ for us, we let this love pour out to everyman, our brother. We cannot run to all parts of the world to bind up the wounds of the sick of body or assist the mentally disturbed, but the contemplative soul in deep prayer before the throne of the Father is exercising the healing power of Jesus Christ. We render Jesus Christ present again in the world in His priestly action of offering the whole world, healed and restored, back to His Father in praise and thanksgiving.

Jesus Christ waits for us to pronounce His Name and render Him again present and localized in our world. Jesus is the Incarnate Word, the plentitude of God's Speech. Mary, the Mother of God, first pronounced His Name, and

He became man, our brother. We, too, have this awesome power, given in embryonic form in our Baptism, a power that increases each time we utter His sacred Name consciously and with reverence and love. We render Jesus Christ present in a new and wonderful way. The world will be little aware of His presence if we are of little faith. As we pronounce this Name we must experience more and more that which Paul prayed all Christians might know:

> Out of His infinite glory, may He give you the power through His Spirit for your hidden self to grow strong, so that Christ may live in your hearts through faith, and then, planted in love and built on love, you will with all saints have strength to grasp the breadth and the length, the height and the depth; until, knowing the love of Christ, which is beyond all knowledge, you are filled with the utter fullness of God. (Ephes. 3:16-19).

Jesus is seeking admission into the hearts of all men. If we cry out in true sincerity, "Lord Jesus, have mercy!" then the words of Revelation will come true: "Look, I am standing at the door, knocking. If one of you hears me calling and opens the door, I will come in to share his meal, side by side with him" (Rev. 3, 20).

THE TRANSFIGURING LORD

Jesus is the transfiguring Lord. He first transfigures us, bathes us in the Taboric Light. It was this light that the Greek Hesychastic Fathers experienced as the enveloping uncreated Energies of the Son and the Spirit assimilating them into divinized beings, one with the Father in Jesus through His Spirit. Then Jesus wishes to transfigure the whole world through us, by our humble actions in the world. He fills all things: "the fullness of Him who fills the whole creation" (Ephes. 1, 23). By pronouncing the Holy Name of Jesus we release this transfiguring power. We call Him into being to touch our suffering world groaning in travail. We ask Him to transform the universe, make each human being, each part of God's creation into members of the body of the Risen Lord. In such prayer, redemption is experienced as the process by which Jesus Lord transfigures the world through other loving human beings who let Him have His redeeming way in them. They sing with Him the Hymn of the Universe; they celebrate, using the raw stuff of their daily monotonous lives, Christ's Mass over the world.

This world is not to be annihilated; it is destined to be transfigured into Christ. The Body of Christ is being formed out of the whole of creation, including not only human beings made according to His image and likeness but also a place for the material, sub-human creation. In pronouncing Jesus' Name, we experience the fact that we are "becoming" members of the Body of Christ that is reaching out to the whole universe in order to bring into His divine life. "The whole creation is eagerly waiting for God to reveal His sons" (Rom. 8, 19). In this transfiguring process the whole cosmos will bend before the power of Jesus. "But God raised Him high and gave Him the Name which is above all other names so that *all beings* in the heavens, on earth and in the underworld, should bend the knee at the Name of Jesus and that every tongue should acclaim Jesus Christ as Lord to the glory of God the Father" (Phil. 2:9-11).

In His resurrection appearances to His disciples, Jesus showed Himself in various forms. "After this, He showed Himself under *another* form to two of them as they were on their way into the country" (Mk. 16, 12). He continues to reveal Himself in various forms as the power that is transfiguring this world through us. What higher form of contemplation than consciously to let the transfiguring power of Jesus pour over us and through us to the whole world! What greater sharing in the priesthood of Christ than to pronounce the Sacred Name that transfigures each person that we meet! We serve them in the Name of Jesus. We cry out to the Lord, so that they together with us will reach the fullness of the sons of God. "Come, Lord Jesus, Maranatha!" (Rev. 22, 20). Fill up Your Body with every human being, fashioning one Body, one faith, one Father, one Baptism, one Spirit of love.

The Body of Christ is evolving until all will recognize Him as head of the New Creature, the Body of Christ, the Church whose Head is the Lord Jesus. Thus we move from petition to praise and thanksgiving: the reverent invocation of the Name of Jesus leads us into the continual celebration of the cosmic Eucharist of Jesus Christ. "With desire I have desired to eat this passover with you" (Lk. 22, 15). Jesus celebrates with us His *barakah*, His thanksgiving to the awesome, transcendent Father. And we are given this same power through Jesus Christ to pronounce our *barakah* in praise of the Father. We make Jesus' prayer ours as we pronounce all day the Name of Jesus, the Name that most pleases the Heavenly Father.

The Name of Jesus leads us to the Holy Spirit. Jesus Christ is always sending us the Paraclete in order that we might understand in the heart, not only with the mind, all that Jesus has said, all that He is. St. Paul tells us that without the Holy Spirit we cannot even say the Name of Jesus. The Spirit sent into our hearts teaches us to call out, "Abba, Father," to love the Lord with our whole heart. "Not by bread alone does man live," is a message taught us in the desert of our hearts by the Spirit who drives us there. It is one and the same Spirit who hovered over the chaotic world in the beginning, who hovered over the Israelites in the desert as the cloud by day and the pillar of fire by night, who hovered over the Virgin Mary at Nazareth when she conceived by the Holy Spirit and the Word became flesh, who hovered over the humble suffering Servant of Yahweh when He was baptized in the Jordan, who again hovered in the cloud through which the Father spoke His approving words at the Transfiguration on top of Mount Tabor, "This is my Beloved Son in whom I am well-pleased"; it was the same Spirit who hovered over the Mother of God and the disciples at the first Pentecost in the form of fiery tongues, and the same Holy Spirit hovers over us with His mighty power when we pronounce the sacred Name of Jesus. As we pronounce that Name, the Spirit of Jesus teaches us all we need to know about Him. He pours into our heart His gifts of prayer, faith, healing, prophecy, of speaking in tongues of adoration and glory to the Father, of reading hearts, of discerning God's ways. He fills us with His fruits of love, peace, joy, gentleness, and kindness (Gal. 5, 22).

JESUS LEADS US TO THE FATHER

The chief work of Jesus both on earth and now in His glorious resurrection is to reveal to us the Father. "Philip, he who sees me, sees the Father" (Jn. 14, 9). Jesus is only the Way that leads us to the Father. The Father is greater than Jesus. The Son has His whole reality in being related to the Father. The Word of God has no meaning except in relationship to the One who speaks that Word, namely, the Heavenly Father. The Father is eternally well-pleased in

His Son (Lk. 3, 22) because He is the perfect Image of the Father. The Father sees Himself totally in the Other and loves Him in the outpouring of Himself to the Other through His Spirit of Love. The Father begets us as His children when we unite ourselves with Jesus. We become sons of God and co-heirs with Jesus forever of Heaven.

In leading us to the Father, Jesus brings us into a total presence of God where we experience Him as Love. Sun's rays can flash off a prism and give colored light. The same rays can hit a lens and become concentrated. Not only do they illuminate but they burn with the heat of fire. This is similar to the experience of the continuous repetition, in loving adoration, of the Name of Jesus. The presence of Jesus generates a burning love within our hearts. A unity that simplifies the whole mystery of God's infinite love in the first creation, the incarnation, redemption, and our sanctification, takes over and operates in our hearts. Christ, in Paul's words, "lives in your hearts through faith, and then, planted in love and built on love, you will with all the saints have strength to grasp the breadth and the length, the height and the depth; until, knowing the love of Christ, which is beyond all knowledge, you are filled with the utter fullness of God" (Ephes. 3:17-19).

We begin to experience how Jesus gathers all things together. The whole Christ comes to us through the revelation of the Spirit as our Alpha and Omega, our beginning and our end. The mere Name is not important. It is the presence that flows from the recitation of the Name. Hence the Jesus Prayer is more than an ejaculation, a spiritual opiate to use, as Franny in John Salinger's novel sought to do, in order to "cop out" of society or to run away into a dream world of escape and uninvolvement.

Synchronizing this Name with our breath, we know by experience that He is our breath, our very life. Our "magnificent obsession" becomes the consciousness of His increasing and our proportionate decreasing before His allness. Only the Holy Spirit can lead us into that intimate, mysterious knowledge which Paul wanted to possess; "All I want is to know Christ and the power of His resurrection and to share His sufferings by reproducing the pattern of His death" (Phil. 3, 10).

THE JESUS PRAYER—A WAY OF LIFE

The Jesus Prayer is ultimately a way of life in Christ, the life which St. Paul so dynamically describes in his epistles. This is a life in a Person who dwells intimately and deeply within us. He gives us the power to become sons of God, to love the Father with His love. We experience grace no longer as a thing, but rather as a relation in love to Persons, to the uncreated Energies, Jesus Christ and His Spirit, loving the Father in us. The Name of Jesus brings God's presence into our life. His is an active presence of love that continues to love His world through us and to change His creation into a new and transfigured world.

Today we are experiencing the trauma of reexamining the traditional forms of our faith. We must return to the experience of a heartfelt encounter with Jesus the living Lord. His presence can no longer be for us a mere thing. We can no longer be content to be a subject adoring a far-off object. We have been freed by Christ's Spirit and are no longer under the law of sin. "Everyone moved by the Spirit is a son of God. The spirit you received is not the spirit of slaves bringing fear into your lives again; it is the spirit of sons, and it makes us cry out, 'Abba, Father!'

The Spirit Himself and our spirit bear united witness that we are children of God " (Rom. 8:14-16).

Dostoevsky in his novel, *Brothers Karamazov,* has given one of the most severe indictments against the Catholic Church ever found in literature. What he said could also apply to the Orthodox or any traditional Protestant Church that has bound itself too long within the extrinsic forms of "churchiness," having departed from the actual charismatic event of Jesus Christ from whom all Christian forms of worship and doctrine have their beginning and meaning. In his *Legend of the Grand Inquisitor,* Dostoevsky, through Ivan Karamazov, tells the story about Christ returning to earth and appearing in Seville at the time of the Holy Inquisition. After performing a miracle, Christ is imprisoned and sentenced by the Inquisitor to be burned at the stake the next day. The latter visits the Prisoner at night. (I do not wish to enter into the polemics that were in the intention of the author, but in general Dostoevsky was attacking a formalized religion that was leading the masses of people like sheep, by taking from them the terrible responsibility of using their free choice and judgment to choose Christ). The Grand Inquisitor tells his Prisoner:

> We have corrected Thy work and have founded it upon miracle, mystery and authority. And men rejoiced that they were again led like sheep and that the terrible gift that had brought them such suffering was, at last, lifted from their hearts.

Christ is branded by the Inquisitor as the greatest enemy of mankind, because He brings to men His terrible gift of inner freedom. That is why the Grand Inquisitor is determined to burn Him, in order to save humanity from

His influence once and for all. The Inquisitor promises that he will burn the Christ on the following day and guarantees that Christ's obedient flock, at a sign from the Inquisitor, will heap the hot coals around the pile on which He will be burned. Without uttering a word, Christ goes up to him and kisses him on his pale and bloodless lips. The Inquisitor shudders. Then he opens the prison door: "Go, and come no more. . .come not at all, never, never." Christ silently goes out and vanishes into the dark alleys of the town. Thus Christ walks out of our lives, driven out because we, our own Inquisitors, prefer to His liberating interior freedom the totalitarian dogmatism of an undisciplined life of self-indulgence. We are afraid to allow Him to make good His statement: "My truth shall make you free." He who is the Way, the Truth, and the Life is not allowed to lead us into the freedom of new creatures, sons of God and heirs of Heaven. Perhaps the best way to call Him back into our empty, frustrated, cold lives is still the way of the early Fathers: "Weap, there is no other way. Lord Jesus Christ, Son of God, have mercy on me a sinner."

5

Man—The Icon of God

In that delightful modern parable entitled *Jonathan Livingston Seagull*[1], an instructing seagull tries to explain: "You've got to understand that a seagull is an unlimited idea of freedom, an image of the Great Gull, and your whole body, from wingtip to wingtip, is nothing more than your thought itself." In another passage the instructing seagull explains what is needed to reach fulfillment as a seagull: ". . .the hardest thing in the world is to convice a bird that he is free and that he can prove it for himself if he'd just spend a little time practicing. Why should that be so hard?"[2]

Man was made by God to be free. This makes him unique among all the other creatures of this universe. Man stands as an intellectual being as the lord and master, capable of controlling the movement of creation. He also stands, as a willing being, ordered towards love, as prophet and priest, capable of communing with his Maker and transfiguring the created elements of the cosmos into signs of his living surrender to his Maker and Father.

Man's uniqueness over all creation consists in his power to be self-positing. Man has been ordered by God's creation to a living dynamic relationship in self-surrendering love to God. He is made, as Genesis (Gen 1 26) says, "according to the Image and Likeness" of God. But, as the Greek Fathers so unanimously insisted along with St. Paul and St. John, *the* Image of God is precisely Jesus Christ, the Word according to whom the whole world has been created. "Through Him and. with Him and in Him. . all glory and honor is Yours, Almighty Father. . ."

Emil Brunner in a very condensed way summarizes the basic theological anthropology around the model of image and likeness in these words:

> God creates man in such a way that in this very creation man is summoned to receive the Word actively, that is, he is called to listen, to understand, and to believe. God creates man's being in such a way that man knows that he is determined and conditioned by God, and in this fact is truly human. The being of man as an 'I' is being from and in the Divine 'Thou,' or, more exactly, from and in the Divine Word, whose claim 'calls' man's being into existence. . .The characteristic imprint of man, however, only develops on the basis of the Divine determination, as an answer to a call, by means of a decision. The necessity for decision, an obligation which he can never evade, is the distinguishing feature of man. . .it is the being created by God to stand 'over-against' Him, who can reply to God, and who in this answer alone fulfills—or destroys—the purpose of God's creation.[3]

A RETURN TO THE EARLY FATHERS

There is a strong renaissance of Christian mysticism developing. There will also be a greater return to the basic insights of the Early Fathers, especially of the Christian East, whose theology was primarily the fruit of their deep, mystical prayer-life. Holy Scripture, especially the writings of St. John and St. Paul, became for them the living Word of God and gave them a solid anthropology as seen from God's viewpoint.

Such charismatic giants, purified by years of monastic asceticism, spoke from their Spirit-filled experiences of divinization *(theosis)*. They experienced in prayer a dynamic process of growth from a potential relationship to God through Jesus Christ to an ever-increasing consciousness of being assimilated into the ocean of God's *allness*. Would it not be profitable for those eager to advance in Christian mysticism to go back to the simple view of the spiritual life as presented by the Early Fathers of the Eastern Churches in order to rediscover points of emphasis lost or at least somewhat de-emphasized by scholastic theologians?

The early Eastern patristic writers developed their whole doctrine of grace, creation, their theological anthropology and psychology of man and therefore their whole understanding of the ascetical life, around the image and likeness doctrine. Among Catholic, Protestant, and Orthodox scholars there is a rebirth of patristic studies, because of the innate conviction that the early Eastern Fathers grasped as in no other age the understanding of the pristine Christianity, especially as expounded in the writings of St. John and St. Paul.

THE END OF THE SPIRITUAL LIFE

Christian spirituality, as it evolved in the early centuries of Christianity, was a practical science, a way of life in God. The articulation of that science followed practical experience. The earliest Christians were mainly concerned with living the new-found faith in simple obedience to the message of the Gospel. In the midst of paganism the followers of Christ gave witness to the "good news" that Jesus Christ came to bring all men. We find a stark living out of the commandments of Christ, especially

those of fraternal charity, without any desire to specu-
late on the *why*. The event that Christ concretized by His
Incarnation was a vivid experience, not only through the
mystical, risen life of Christ living in the souls of His early
followers through grace, but even through a closeness in
time and space to the very historical Person Himself.

Gradually, especially through attempts to explain this
living experience "in Christ" to neighboring pagans and
Jews, or through the effort to preserve the revealed truths
against the attacks of heretical teachings, there arose in the
Church not only Christian philosophers and theologians
but a tradition, accessible to all Christians, of reflective
knowledge concerning man in his relationship to God as to
his last end. Each Christian felt the necessity of living his
faith reflectively and consciously. He had no Christian
heritage or culture that permeated his society at each step
and kept him in a Christian milieu; he had to create this
milieu for himself. And he began this process of Christian
reflection by asking himself what was the end of his life.

The early Christian seized firmly upon this fundamental truth: the end of life is simply *salvation.* The Greek
word for salvation, *soteria,* is rich with nuances that are
lost to us by the simple word, salvation. For Plato this
meant security, a state of prosperity, good health, well-being. In its natural meaning, all men seek salvation insofar as
all men have a natural will, a *physicon thelema,* to seek
their own happiness or well-being. But the pagans did not
agree always as to what made up this goal of all men's
desires. The Epicureans sought their happiness in material
and intellectual pleasures. The Platonists sought it in
contemplation of the eternal Ideas. Stoics strove to acquire
it through the acquisition of virtues and the deadening of
inordinate passions.

The Christian knew that happiness was the fulfillment of the total man, according to the potentialities placed in him by his Creator. Irenaeus described it simply: the glory of God is man living fully. The Christian knew that God did not create potencies except to be fulfilled; seeds to bring forth a hundred-fold, babes to reach the full maturity of sons of God who are to be "filled with the utter fullness of God" (Ephes. 3:19). St. Paul exhorts the early Christians to prepare in this life for the coming of the Lord. "May every part of your being, spirit, soul and body, be preserved blameless for the day when the Lord shall come" (1 Th. 5:23).

Salvation or man's total happiness, total health, total fulfillment, is effected in God and only by God. Plato and the early pagan philosophers at the time of the proximate dawning of Christianity seemed to sense this, as Festugiere writes: "Perfect happiness for human beings is the union with the Ideas or more correctly, with the One, the Good, with God."[4] Still Plato felt that man could attain this state of complete happiness through his own innate powers. Christians, on the contrary, recognized that this was the goal of man, yet the attainment of it was possible only through the grace of God.

THE HESED COVENANT

In the Old Testament, God is praised as the Savior, the Healer, the source of all life who became involved by condescending mercy, not only to protect His chosen faithful, but also to restore them to full prosperity, full heath of mind and body, the full satisfaction of all the desires that the Maker of man had implanted in him. Man's salvation, his happiness on this earth, consists in serving God. The most characteristic trait of the Old Testament and the term most closely related to the concept of grace in the New Testament is that of *hesed,* the condescending merciful love of God in His covenant made with man. *Hesed* made the Israelites approach God with confidence because *hesed* was based on the eternal word of God that He would not turn away from His Chosen People but that He would protect them from all harm and make them prosperous and happy. Paul in his Epistle to the Hebrews gives us the motive for the faith of the great heroes of Israelite history. Abel, Enoch, Noah, Abraham, Isaac, and Jacob believed in the Lord God. Why? Because they were "awaiting the city with foundations whose architect and builder is God" (Hebr. 11; 10).

In the New Testament, this is the basic conviction commented on by the Early Fathers in their writings and in the Eastern Liturgies, namely, that the aim of all human existence is to obtain the salvation that has been promised by God, worked out for us by God and to be found totally in God. It was God, through Jesus Christ, who effected salvation which, viewed negatively, is a liberation from sin and from the power of Satan. Still viewed negatively, salvation is a liberation from fate that had filled the pagans with black pessimism and despair in the face of their inability to cope with the problem of evil and death. The New Testament is still powerful enough to dissipate such fatalism, whether of the pagan Greek tragedian, Euripedes, or the Latin poet, Lucretius, both of whom lamented a new born babe, brought into life only to suffer and to die, or that brand of nihilistic existentialism of modern times (like that of J. P. Sartre) which holds that there is *no exit* from the absurdity into which man is born.

The New Testament revealed to mankind a loving Father in Heaven who permitted evil in order to draw out greater good in His merciful Providence. Salvation is a liberation from the despair of human loneliness by incorporating the individual person into a new society, a community of the People of God, the *koinonia,* that gives the individual Christian a social, spiritual life of unity with his neighbors by the bond of charity in Christ. Salvation, as conceived negatively by the New Testament, is liberation from death by the gift of eschatological life; it is freedom from mortality and corruption, making the Christian enjoy the immortality *(aphtharsia)* of the Risen Savior who conquered death and its sting.

Positively, salvation is the possession of God who alone is the Good. Possessing Him, we possess the happiness for which He created us. St. Gregory of Nyssa writes: "He is happy who possesses all good. Our beatitude consists in the participation of divine happiness."[5] St. Basil in his homily on Psalm 61 runs through all possible objects that in this life could bring us some share of passing happiness and concludes: "Happy is he who puts his joy not in any of these things reckoned as important in this life but only in the one glory that is God. . .We must esteem the passing glories of this life as miserable and consider those as truly happy who place their glory in God."[6] Again Basil summarizes the basic conviction of all true Christians: "The most perfect good is God. All those who seek Him will never lose Him."[7]

CHRISTOCENTRIC

The early Eastern Fathers built up not only a theology of divinization around the two terms from Genesis 1, 26: "Let us make man *according to our image and likeness*" (*eikon* and *homoiosis*), but we find in their speculation about these two concepts the meeting of an integrated theology of Christ and the Trinity, creation and man, as well as a religious psychology of man, and a dynamic expression of the life of grace.

The Septuagint or Greek Old Testament does not say that man is the image and likeness of God. Man is made only *according to* the image, i.e., in Greek, *kat'eikona.* St. Paul tells us that Jesus Christ

> . . .is the Image of the unseen God and the first-born of all creation, for in Him were created all things in heaven and on earth: Everything visible and everything invisible. . .All things were created through Him and for Him. Before anything was created He existed, and He holds all things in unity. . .Because God wanted all perfection to be found in Him and all things to be reconciled through Him and for Him, when He made peace by His death on the Cross (Col. 1; 15-20).

Jesus Christ is the fullness of God's life, the *Pleroma* of whom we have even in this life received a share. Christ is in some way the total gospel, the New Creation. This seems so evident to any Christian, so we would not be surprised to find this the central point in the early Christian writings. This teaching is exemplified in the lives of the early martyrs who believed that suffering for and with Christ gave them an intimate union with Him. St. Ignatius of Antioch writes to the Romans: "I am now beginning to be a disciple."[8] He wishes to die, to be ground up in order to be made into the bread of Christ. Thus martyrdom was regarded as the surest means to union with Christ; it was looked upon as the height of Christian perfection. "No greater love does man have than to lay down his life for a friend," the Master Himself had said.

When martyrdom ceased to be a common experience in the Christian Church, the Christian writers developed a theology of salvation centered on Christ's recapitulating activities in the universe. Irenaeus is the first to introduce the principle of *anakephalaiosis* or recapitulation in Christ as an integrating structure by which he could explain to the Gnostic heretics and his own flock at Lyons the immanence of Christ in the material world. God became man that man might become God. Jesus Christ is God's Logos, and in Him God is gathering up His entire work, fulfilling it according to His original plan. Christ's work and the whole *real* progress in the universe are measured in terms of the restoration of the first creation through Christ's activities in the cosmos. Irenaeus puts the end of man and the universe simply in the following words:

> For this is why the Word of God is man, and this is why the Son of God became the Son of Man, that man might possess the Word, receive adoption, and become the son of God. In no other way could we receive incorruptibility and immortality except by being united with incorruptibility and immortality. But how could we be united with incorruptibility and immortality, unless incorruptibility and immortality had first become what we are, in order that what is corruptible might be absorbed by incorruptibility and what is mortal by immortality, that so we might receive the adoption of sons?[9]

SALVATION ONLY THROUGH CHRIST

Acts, 4, 12 insists that "no other name under Heaven has been given to men by which we must be saved." Against such heresies as Doceticism, Gnosticism, and the Christological errors of Arianism, Nestorianism and Monophysitism, there was a strenuous battle of words to retain the full Christ and the centrality of His actions in and through us for our salvation. Correct thinking on our salvation was intimately tied up with correct notions on the fundamental truth of Christianity, that of the Incarnation and Person of Jesus Christ. St. Gregory of Nyssa summarizes the Person of Christ in regard to our imitation and adoration of Him:

> The true Christian characteristics are all those which we have been considering about Christ; of these we imitate those qualities of Christ that we are capable of imitating; those others which we are unable to imitate we venerate and adore. [10]

Thus imitation of Christ, according to whose image man has been created, is the constant spiritual task of Christians. Paul's exhortation, "Be imitators of me as I am of Christ," indicates the way of virtues that leads to salvation, that transforms the image within man into the likeness.

If Christians were enjoined by their Founder to be perfect as their Heavenly Father was perfect, how much more readily would they find the way, the truth, and the life of that perfection that was closed to human eyes but opened to them in the Incarnate Person of Jesus Christ? For the first three centuries the imitation of Christ was the center of Christian living. The whole doctrine of imitation of Christ is intimately united with the doctrine of the early Greek Fathers on the image and likeness of God in man. This doctrine was conceived as a theological model in order to describe in biblical terms the dynamic progression towards greater Christian perfection and finally to salvation. This progression is the movement from the ontological image implanted in each human being in creation to a greater likeness where the lineaments of Christ are conceived as hidden in embryonic form in each man by natural creation.

Through Baptism, the Holy Eucharist, and other sacraments, plus a lifetime of virtuous acts performed under the influence of Divine Life, the embryonic form of the image of Christ grows into a fuller likeness to Him. From a basic orientation towards a vital, loving relationship to Christ Jesus living within the Christian, man moves into a greater consciousness of that abiding presence and learns through virtues cultivated over long years and through the power of grace through the sacraments how to yield himself more and more completely to the dominance of Jesus the Lord.

IN THE HOLY SPIRIT

This process of growth in Christ is effected by the Holy Spirit, who is the Life-giver, the *zoopoion,* the maker of Life. Whatever the Church does by way of sanctifying its members in Christ, it does through the Holy Spirit. "No one," says St. Paul, "can say 'Jesus is Lord' except under the influence of the Holy Spirit." St. Basil, in refuting the *Pneumatomachoi* or heretics who denied the divinity of the Holy Spirit, insists on His role as Sanctifier, a role which would not be possible if the Holy Spirit were not also God. "The economy of salvation established for man through the magnificent God and Savior Jesus Christ (Titus, 2, 13) will reach its full realization through the grace of the Spirit." [11] St. Athanasius also insists on the life-giving activity of the Holy Spirit. "The Father through the Word in the Holy Spirit does all things." [12]

The word *spiritual* has lost today its fundamental root meaning in relation to the Holy Spirit. For the early Christians *spiritual* meant not only some immaterial quality, but an effect that was dependent in origin and continuation on the Holy Spirit. We can see this in the meaning applied to a spiritual father, a guide in the spiritual life. As the Spirit brings one to perfection, so the *spiritual* man is the perfect man. Only a spiritualized man, one in whom the Holy Spirit lived and acted, can discourse about God and give guidance in the spiritual life. Similarly, the theologians are those who, under the illumination received from the Holy Spirit, after a long purification and asceticism as preparation, write and discourse about God.

Thus we see that Eastern Christian spirituality is deeply rooted in the central faith of the Holy Trinity. God, the source of all existence, created man according to the image and likeness that is Jesus. The process of moving into a more conscious, loving relationship to God the Father, which means an ontological life of Christ living with man, is effected through the sanctifying activity of the Holy Spirit. St. Cyril of Alexandria shows, however, that these actions and operations of bringing man into the fullness of his powers are effected by the whole Trinity: "All things come from the Father through the Son in the Holy Spirit."[13] Nothing of divine operation is attributed to any Person of the Trinity unless it responds to the inter-Trinitarian relations.[14]

ALL CHRISTIANS ARE MONKS

The process of moving from image to likeness in divinization is the end therefore of every human being. The Fathers did not hold a distinction between precepts of obligation, binding all Christians, and evangelical counsels which are followed only by monks. St. Basil, St. John Chrysostom and others insisted that all Christians are *"monotropi,"* all are monks (from the word *monachos,* the

Christian or human being who became an integrated, whole person). All Christians are to live by one and the same desire for the same goal. St. Gregory of Nyssa says that "there is only one vocation given to all those who believe in Him...that is to be called Christians." [15]

Thus in the matter of perfection there is no distinction between men, women and children, healthy and sick physically, rich and poor materially. St. John Chrysostom emphasizes with great ardor this point:

> The Holy Scriptures do not know any such distinctions. They enjoin that all lead the life of the monks even if they are married. Listen to what Paul says (and when I say Paul, I say also Christ) in writing to married men who have children. He demands from them the same rigorous observance as that demanded from monks. He removes all luxury in their dress and food in writing: 'Women are to pray, decently attired, adorning themselves with modesty and restraint, not with braided hair, gold, pearls, or expensive clothing, but with good deeds as befits women who make profession of worshipping God' (I Tim. 2, 9). And again: 'She who gives herself up to pleasure is dead while she is still alive' (I Tim. 5, 6). And again: 'If then we have something with which we can nourish and clothe ourselves, let us be content with it' (I Tim. 6, 8). What could we demand more of from the monks? [16]

MAN—THE IMAGE OF GOD'S INEXPRESSIBLE GLORY

We have no doubt obscured many of the central issues in Christianity. By going back to the Christian Fathers we can once again seize that one great thing, the *unum necessarium,* and then let everything else fall into place. But we have to ground ourselves solidly in the one fundamental truth of why God created us. The early Christians had the tremendous conviction that Christ is the image of the Father and that we have been created according to His image.

Our whole fullness and perfection reside in an assimilation to the likeness of Christ. But it is not just Christ as a moral example outside of us, but Christ dynamically, ontologically living in us and working in us through this grace. Grace for them is no longer a thing; it is an encounter with the living Person whose life is in us, acting to deify us. When this concept is understood, then one can grasp the wealth of doctrine, not only in St. John, but above all in St. Paul who is constantly writing about being "in Christ, " as in the unity of a single, living person effected through an *organic* union between two persons, Christ and the individual; yet each retains his own individual nature.

So this image that has been made by God has been distorted by sin, but it can never be destroyed. This image resides in man insofar as he has an intellect and a will in his very nature; therefore it can never be taken away. No matter how much a man may sin, this image will always remain. We have in the Eastern Byzantine funeral service for a layman this phrase, "I am the image of Thine inexpressible glory even though I bear the wounds of sin." So, God's image may be covered over; it may not be truly operating to the fullest of its powers; but it can never be obliterated, never be completely destroyed. This is the way God created us and He can never take back His creation. We have been made according to the image of God; so no power on earth, not even God Himself, can destroy what He has created. This would be to go against His own will. So the whole aim of the Christian life is precisely to allow this seed of deification, filiation in Christ, to be developed through a lifetime of submitting to the will of God.

Athanasius (and Irenaeus said the same before him) stated that God became man in order that man might become God.[17] This was meant literally, not that we become by *nature* God, but, as St. Peter says in his Second Epistle we are "participators in the divine nature."[18] This is the great truth that the early Christians seized, and this is what made them so optimistic and so joyful in regard to God's created universe. In a pagan world where there was much pessimism and fatalism, the non-Christians did not know why they were living. "Where are we going?" they despondently asked. But Christ truly came to give us this tremendous revelation: that God so loved us as to give us the possibility of becoming truly sons of God.

St. John, in the 17th Chapter of his Gospel, says that Our Lord prayed at the Last Supper, "May they all be one as Thou, Father, art in me, and I in Thee, so also may they be one in us." We know by this grace of the indwelling Trinity that precisely only through the Cross leading to the resurrection could Christ be glorified in His humanity so that He could transcend all matter, all space and all time and truly come into us and live. Had He not died, had He not risen, this would not have been possible. Thus the whole Christian life is centered around the death of Christ, but always leading to His resurrection which makes it therefore possible that this new life is brought to us.

St. Maximus the Confessor has written a great deal about the mystery of the Trinity living within us. "God and those who are worthy of God have one and the same energy," he says.[19] It is not that we lose our free will, but through the mutual operation of God and man, there comes about a union of these two wills. "We remain creatures," he says, "while becoming God by grace."[20] The deification of man is something that does not touch merely our will or our soul, but it touches the whole of our being.

This is something which Gregory Palamas insisted upon strongly, and in this regard he was merely repeating what all the Fathers had said against the Gnostics, who spurned matter. Under the great influence of Platonism, too, there was, especially in Origen, a tendency to downgrade the body. St. Paul, however, in I Corinthians, exalts the body. "Your body is the temple of the Holy Spirit." Once Christ took on a human body, He brought about the possibility of contact not just with souls but with our own body, with the whole material world; and thus we can understand the cosmic dimensions of St. Paul, his teaching that it is not just the soul, but it is the whole created world which has come from God and which yearns to return to Him. It is groaning in travail until it be brought to its completion, and that completion could never have been brought about unless Christ had touched man and this material world through a material body. That body glorified in the life of the resurrection now lives inmanently in this universe, working to bring it to its fulfillment. So Christ really did not ascend "up there," wherever that is, but His ascension merely serves as an image of His deification or transfiguration of His material body. It is the same body but now spiritualized and able to transcend matter, space and time, and thus it can truly be immanent in this whole material universe and bring the cosmos to its proper completion.

COSMIC REDEMPTION

This whole idea of the cosmic redemption is one that is very prevalent in the Eastern Fathers, and we find this same concept expressed in the attitude of the East towards relics and icons. Matter is not evil; it came from God and can serve as a touchstone for contact with God. Christ took on a body, and it was through His body that He made contact with other human beings. It was through his saliva and the touch of his hands, with words, gestures and material objects like bread and wine, that He brought this divine life to other human beings. So, too, this whole universe is now, we might say, a living sacrament (if we use the word sacrament in a broad sense), a possible meeting of man and God whereby this not only symbolizes, but it actually effects that divine life. We see, for instance with regard to the devotion to relics, that we in the West, especially of the Anglo-Saxon mentality, feel an innate abhorrence to the veneration of a bone, a tooth, a piece of hair. We revolt somehow at looking at a skull, and when we do, we see only a skull. The Eastern Christian could see something beyond this. Oriental Christians have this wonderful ability of seeing beyond the surface. And here we enter the whole realm of symbolism that is so strong in the East. A relic is a sign leading to a greater reality; hence it really does not make much difference whether a skull or a tooth really came from this or that Saint to whom it is attributed. The point is that this relic is a sign of a temple of God that lived on this earth and in whom the Holy Spirit lived and worked and that one day will be glorified as the body of Christ is now glorified. This human body will live forever in the spiritual life of the hereafter. When we take this attitude, therefore, the material world takes on a different meaning and perspective.

The early Fathers, in asking this question: "What is the nature of man?" turned not to man's puny mind and his speculation to find an answer, but they turned to God Himself. They listened to God as He spoke in the very first book of Genesis: "And God said: Let us make man according to our image and likeness."[21] Here we find the Biblical phrases in Greek *kat' eikona* (according to the image) and the second phrase *kath' homoiosin* (according to the likeness). We find that this language was in fact already used by the pagans, especially the Greeks; hence whoever wrote this phrase of Genesis was using a philosophical language already common to Middle-or Neo-Platonism. To approach the image or *eikon* was, in Plato's writings, the end of man. Man was made according to this image that existed in the abstract idea and was to become as far as possible the likeness of God Himself.[22] Hence this vocabulary was already worked out in the pagan world, but the real ontological possibility of bringing to fruition what the vocabularly expressed was never reached.

The pagans never dreamed for a moment that there could be a real, ontological evolution into a likeness of God. The Fathers used the terms borrowed from the philosophers, but only through the Scriptural revelation that guided their speculation. For instance, they used other texts, such as, "Be ye perfect, as your Heavenly Father is perfect," an injunction on the part of Christ, that we progress to a greater perfection, to a similarity to God Himself; as well as the text, "Through faith in Jesus Christ you are all now God's Sons," and St. John's "We are sons of God even now." Thus this pagan background of philosophical speculation plus revelation gave them the framework for working out an anthropology of man. Christ is the perfect image; Paul says, "He is the image of the invisible God." And we have been created, not in the image of God, but *kat' eikona* according to the image. So, actually, this *eikon* the image, is Christ Himself, and we have been created according to His image. We have our meaning, our being in Christ, as St. Paul says, "In Him in whom we move and breathe and have our being." So our whole fulfillment is centered around Christ. If man has been made by God to Christ's image and likeness, where, therefore, do we find this image and likeness in man? Is the *image* of God in man different from the *likeness?* Is there a progression?

Here one must not lose patience with the Fathers. One Father may interpret this phrase, *image,* as the total, ontological, created being that can never be destroyed and *likeness* as the area of what we would call grace—the supernatural elevation that can be lost. However, this is inserted into the natural created being, by a free, gratuitous gift of God. In the 4th century, St. Epiphanius, a very outspoken character, says impatiently, "Where the image is and in what it consists, God alone knows, but we should admit the image *(kat' eikona)* in man lest we appear to reject God's gift and refuse to believe Him."[23] But when we begin to examine the individual writings of these Fathers we find a great confusion, because on one page they write about the image as distinct from the likeness, while on another page they write about the image getting always brighter and brighter, or they state that it was lost by sin or covered over by sin.

A PROCESS OF GROWTH

Actually, there is no contradiction. These are very fluid concepts and only from the context can one understand what the individual writer is trying to say. But by and large, there is among the Fathers the basic conviction of the spiritual life as a progressive development of the image and likeness from the very moment that we

are born to the moment that we die. There is a constant
movement from birth to the beatific vision. In our birth
we receive the *kat' eikona* and it can never be lost. But the
moment that we are baptized we receive the *kath'
homoiosin* but in a very embryonic form. As we progress
this grows into greater stature and vibrancy. But it can be
lost anywhere along the line if instead of progressing
constantly towards God we should wilfully turn away
from God and move away from life (but always eschatological divine life) towards death. This death is not
physical death, as we mentioned before, but it is the death
of God's own life in us. Sin takes us away from this life.
But we always have, as a substratum, this *kat' eikona* even
though we are moving away from the likeness of God. The
image can never be destroyed.

This image would consist, therefore, in our ability,
through our intellect and our will, to respond to God in
His invitation to return to Him. So in this regard we are
one with Christ. In His pre-existent stage as the Son of
God in the Triadic life, He was the perfect image of His
Father. He is the speech that reflected perfectly the mind
of the Father. And as man also He is our image, according
to which we have been created, both in having an intellect
and a will and in our whole being, including our physical
body. Actually, the formality that makes up this *eikon*
would be that quality, parallel to our own nature, that we
find in Christ and that makes Him truly the image of His
Father, that is, the free will of Christ to respond to His
Heavenly Father, to say "Yes, Father." And man will
always have this freedom; he can never lose the possibility
of responding to God. So, no matter how great a sinner a
man may be, in whom there is no life or likeness to God,
there will always be this basic ability to respond to God, to

recover again, with God's mercy and grace, the life and the likeness to Him.

St. Irenaeus is the first great Father who develops this doctrine, and he clearly distinguishes, as I mentioned, that the image is the ontological structure of man and the likeness is in the area of grace that can be lost. The first is an *imago in plasmate* as he calls it, and that is present in man in his very creation, while the other is the *similitudo per Spiritum*.[24] Irenaeus, as all the Fathers do, follows St. Paul in maintaining that man is made up of body, soul, and Spirit. The Spirit is not present when man is born, but, for Paul and the early Fathers, the Spirit was considered as a part of his perfect nature. This is a concept that is quite different from that of the West. We would never say that man's nature is to have God's life. But the early Fathers saw that God created man not only with a body and soul, but God also placed man in a movement towards this divine life, the Spirit. The fact that he does not have that Spirit in him does not say that he is malformed; it merely says that he is not yet living according to his full nature.

So, following St. Irenaeus, we find other Fathers like Sts. Athanasius and Basil, Gregory of Nazianzen and Cyril of Alexandria, who maintain this clear distinction between the ontological image and the area of grace, an accidental perfection that is acquired and can be lost. The Alexandrian school, on the other hand, a more intellectual tradition as exemplified by Clement of Alexandria and Origen, usually ignored the ontological distinction. These writers put the divine image in the moral order. Thus man's image of God by nature (intellect and will) is something that is perfected through moral actions modelled on the image of Christ. It is an area of constant progress, but there is no clear-cut distinction between that which can be lost and that which can be gained. I think the Alexandrian writers who speak only of an image and seemingly pass over the duality between nature and supernatural elevation admit a progressive development in which this image becomes more vibrant. The image is present but is always growing into a greater similitude to the image of Christ. So there is no contradiction at all; the different emphasis depends on the writer and the scope of his writings. If he is a moralist like St. John Chrysostom or Origen, he seeks to give us a model, Christ; thus Christ is the image, and we are moving constantly toward becoming an image of God. So there would not be the emphasis on an ontological created image; rather, we are progressing towards the divine image. But actually they are saying one and the same thing as Irenaeus.

THE PATRISTIC CONCEPT OF NATURE

I mentioned before that the early Fathers conceive nature as the total being, created as body and soul along with an orientation towards the divine life, and all this was included in the one general word *physis* (nature). *Physis* is a broader term than our "nature." It embraces not only the nature of man as it comes from the hand of God, but it also looks towards its completion and is defined according to its fulfillment rather than the beginning stage. Thus *physis* is everything that God puts into man, whether it is in the beginning stage or the final one, and it also includes that which comes to man after he is baptized and begins to lead a virtuous life.

The Fathers consider, therefore, everything in nature or that comes to nature after baptism as *kata physin* (according to nature); all is within the structure of nature.

There is nothing superimposed upon nature; rather patristic doctrine emphasizes the idea of a dynamic drawing out of the potencies present in the first creation, and the expression *hyper physin* (above nature, super-nature) is never used. "Super-nature" refers to the area of the extraordinary, irregular, almost magical, but the term is not used in the Western sense, as something superimposed upon nature. Such a concept is totally unknown in the Fathers. But the term parallel to *kata physin* is *para physin* (against nature), referring to the area of sin. Anything that is *para physin* is against nature or outside of it, but it never coincides with nature. Everything in man that is given to him in his creation or that comes after is *kata physin* and is *good*. So, even our passions, as everything that we have from God, are *good*.

Now, how do we explain evil? Evil, for the Fathers, is something that has to come from outside of God's creation, that is to say, outside of man's own nature. Therefore they had a very dynamic view of sin as almost personalized, such as we find in St. Paul. The fallen angel, Satan himself, becomes the instigator of evil. Evil thus comes, not from man's basic nature that is good, but it comes from outside us and touches our intellect and our will. We may succumb to evil, but it never is able to touch and destroy or corrupt our nature. We can lose grace, the divine similitude, but the nature given to us by God is good and can never be destroyed. The will, therefore, is the great determining factor. There are two parts in the human will. The first is *autexousion* (self-possession). Man is determined by himself, not by any outside agent. He is free, completely autonomous. Now, this autonomy can never be destroyed. Man is always intrinsically master of his own destiny. No outside agent coming in and touching his nature can ever determine him, but he himself must determine, in the face of temptation, to succumb or not.

The other part of his free will is *eleutheria. Eleutheria* is that quality which we would perhaps call the "integrated nature." Man, the total man, reacts according to his total nature for his total fulfillment: this is our integrated nature, with no division and no disorientation from God. The whole being harmoniously reacts according to the powers which God has given it. Now, in the first sin man lost this *eleutheria,* this harmony among all his powers, so that the passions, the intellect, the will, the imagination, the external senses all tended toward their own proper ends and unity was lost.

Christ came and presented Himself as the perfect man. Christ is Adam, the second and *perfect* man. He reconciled in Himself the two parts of the human will. He freely determined Himself, as all of us do, but He possesses in His humanity this perfect integrated nature. He comes to give us that quality whereby we can be restored. This restoration is expressed in the familiar term if St. Paul and repeated by Origen and Irenaeus, *anakephalaiosis* (recapit-ulation): we are restored to the head. Christ is our head and we return, through grace, to Him, and thereby we become a unity again, but a unity in Christ. It is in being restored to Christ that we find our full freedom. Now we begin to see how, in the beatific vision, we will have perfect freedom and yet we will never be able to sin. We will always be determining ourselves towards our fulfill-ment. There will be perfect integration among all our members, we will choose always that which is *kata physin* and never the possibility of going *para physin* (against nature). What happened after sin when man turned away from God was, as I said, this disorientation, this dis-harmony introduced into our passions.

We find, for instance, Evagrius saying that from nature no evil could enter; no evil thought could enter, because we were not in the beginning created evil. Rather, the Lord sowed good seed in His field; evil comes from outside. We find Nilus, one of the great early monks of the desert, writing in his *Sermo Asceticus* about the infiltra-tion of evil into man's nature from outside. "God gave the command to do good and to avoid sin, but opposing powers make us tend toward evil, and it becomes difficult to do this good. These sinful powers are not innate to man's nature, but they are brought in from outside." [25] Macarius says in regard to the *passions* (and we must recall that when they used this word they were not talking about our irascible and concupiscible passions that constitute part of our nature; rather they were considering the passions as now disoriented through the loss of *eleutheria*): "Therefore, he who says that the cause of the ignominy of the passions is that they are from nature and not accidents has changed the truth of God into a real lie. As I said above, the immaculate and pure God prepared man's image to His own, but by the jealousy of the Devil death entered into the world. From these words of Christ 'every planting not done by my Father will be uprooted,' and, because every creature of God is good, learn that the passions rooted in us are not ours but come from others." [26]

And so, it is only natural that the Fathers would look upon the spiritual life, the recovering of the divine life in man's nature, as a warfare against the evil one who is trying to drive this life out of us. This concept is on every page of St. Paul; we find it also in the Synoptics. Likewise, St. Peter warns us that "the devil goes about like a roaring lion seeking whom he may devour." Life is conceived as a battle, a struggle against the evil one, and Christ opposes that evil one. We are in the middle, yet no one can touch us, not even Christ, not even the devil, unless we really want to yield ourselves to the one or the other. The whole ascetical life is patterned on the idea of restoring our being and acting in Christ, so that the disharmony which allows all our faculties to go out for their own proper ends is removed, and man is brought back now into a harmonious *being,* an integrated being, a reintegration into Christ.

THE ROLE OF CHRIST

Irenaeus is the first of the Fathers to give us a real Christology. He speaks of the Incarnation as the necessary means to bring about the salvation that man himself could never attain. The Word of God was made a Son of Man in order that man might become God. He had to become all things to man except sin; so He comes as the perfect image of God and He gives us the possibility of restoring the likeness of God in our souls, in our whole being. It is not just our soul that becomes the temple of God, but our whole being must be refashioned "according to Christ." Man must be ontologically united with Christ's life within Him. In this teaching, Irenaeus very nicely unites the mysticism of both St. John and St. Paul. He identifies the flesh of Christ with ours and states that the promise of eternal life is given us because Christ is the prince of life.

Later Origen develops this same image, but with him, Christ is more the moral example, the teacher, the *pedagogos* who draws us by His example. He does not stress, as Irenaeus and the whole Antiochene school did, that ontological life which Christ came to give us, which is in us by Baptism and which is developed by virtuous living. So in the Antiochene school we find this doctrine highly developed in the sense of a dynamic growth, similar to a seed growing into its fruition. According to the more "intellectual" school of Alexandria, the emphasis is on the mind contemplating the example of Christ, listening to the inner voice, the inner speech of God which is Christ within us, and responding by a virtuous life. Athanasius summarizes Irenaeus's approach when he says, "The Divine Word was made man that we might become gods," [27] and from then on all the Fathers repeat this phrase. Christ was made visible in His body in order that we might have an idea of the invisible Father. Christ is the image of the invisible God. He has supported the outrages of men in order that we might have a part in His immortality.

St. Gregory of Nyssa develops a sacramental theology but one much different from our own, which is so heavily constructed along the lines of Aristotelian causality. For Gregory it is each sacrament that gives us a greater movement, an impetus towards this proximity to God in His own life. So Baptism purifies man from this sin and from death, and puts man on the road back to God's likeness. The Eucharist unites our being with the total Christ; He comes to *us* as a total being, and therefore He is exerting, if we only allow Him, an influence on *all* the parts of our being, in order to reintegrate our total being in Himself. So He is concerned with how we use our eyes, our ears and everything else, that gradually we may see, as St. Paul says, that "whatsoever you do, whether you are eating or drinking" all has meaning in Christ, and that meaning derives from contact with Christ in the Eucharist. This union develops throughout the day, so that gradually there is no longer a dichotomy in us; we see that Christ is not interested merely in our soul but that He is vitally interested in our *whole* being. Gradually the dichotomy between action and contemplation disappears.

In a very summary fashion we have tried to present here the main lines of the patristic anthropology of man's nature, built around the image and likeness concept from Genesis. Father H. Crouzel, S.J., has written an excellent work on the image of God in Origen, [28] in which he says that Origen's concept offers a synthesis of all the theology of the Fathers. Here we find man's creation conceived as a movement towards God, including the fall, the sin of man, and then the Incarnation of Christ and His restoration of man in the sonship of God. Origen highlights the ever progressing movement of sanctification through the Holy Spirit working in the human soul in order to refashion it according to the image of Christ. So we have here an ontological dynamism that is solidly based on Scripture, especially St. John and St. Paul, and that gives us practical applications in our daily life, since we really need an integrating, simple figure around which we can build our spiritual life. But we must not be content with this synthesis, for there are certainly lacunae and deficiencies in it. The Fathers use metaphors like image, likeness, model, mirror, light, rays, and so on, and this could constitute a mere verbalism through a lack of precision in speech. We need to supplement this theology of the Eastern Fathers with some of the deeper insights of Western theology. St. Augustine developed to a high degree a theory of the image and likeness, as did also St. Thomas Aquinas. From them we learn certain clear distinctions that we must keep in mind. We can learn from the Fathers to have an integrated and very dynamic view of the whole, but we can avoid confusion if we have these other distinctions clearly in mind.

We see that the doctrine of the Eastern Fathers flows directly from Scripture. In a very true sense, as God has conceived man, he is truly man only when he emerges from himself and returns to his true self, and that means turning to Him who is the perfect image of His Father. We can find, I think, in our daily modern life many applications of this doctrine of the image and likeness. It will certainly recover for us a more existential or ontological view of the life of God in our soul. I believe we can rediscover a more dynamic view of grace, of God's working within us, of a personal encounter with Christ living in us ontologically with His own life—drawing our whole being, not just our soul or our intellect, to Himself. He is interested in our whole, total being and therefore we should yield ourselves constantly to His influence, to His presence, to His activity, so that He may integrate us in Himself. We must put on the mind of Christ. We can profit a great deal from this single-mindedness of the early Christians in order to sift through the accretions of many centuries of theological speculation and to seize on the *unum necessarium* and set about with no side distractions to obtain this pearl of great price.

God has created us with a basic drive towards union with Him. We find this in so many atheists. They are searching and they do not know why. God has implanted in every man this yearning, this drive, this image that will only be satisfied in the full fruition as a son of God. And when man keeps suppressing this basic image and these drives by substituting creatures which will never really satisfy his yearning as only God can, then our hearts are truly restless until they rest in God, as St. Augustine said for every man. Augustine's phrase beautifully summarizes the dynamic concept of the image and likeness of God in man.

With our emphasis today on more personalism, we can see God's personal love, His activity for us, His invitation, not just in a grand moment of our life when we decide to follow God more perfectly in our chosen state of life, but in every moment. God is working dynamically to bring us to that end for which He created us. Therefore, every moment is a constant vocation: *Deus vocat.* His invitation is extended constantly to us, calling us to actuate this image into a greater likeness, to become more like His Son through grace, in the life of the resurrection that God gives us in embryo through Baptism. Thus man is more precisely an image to the image of Christ. This image consists in man's having an intellect and a will by which he can, by reflective consciousness, respond to the mind of God and put on Christ Himself through his union with Christ in virtuous living. We are not just performing actions and practicing virtues by ourselves, but there is developed a true *synergy,* a union with Christ, and together we are living our lives in a constant glory to God in the highest. So the likeness is that same movement in a greater degree of union.

We do not wait until the beatific vision to aspire to this union. We have it even now as we go through our daily lives, through our virtuous acts. There are two persons, but they are so intimately united by grace, by our loving submission to Christ, that there becomes one will. "I live now, not I" means not I as an independent person without reference at all to God, but I live "now, not I, but Christ lives in me." I become very conscious of this union and this union spills out into action. Contemplation and action blend together so that I really create, as Teilhard de Chardin has said, a *divine milieu.* Wherever I am, the whole universe is truly a temple of God, and I find God everywhere and in all things dynamically working to bring me and the whole universe to Christ. I am not alone, but I am a part of this total cosmos, and I will find my completion precisely in my activity in this world. I go to God together with this whole wonderful world of ours. The world does not become a hindrance, but it is rather the instrument through which I can respond to God, and, in listening to His call and accepting it, I can move from image to likeness.

6

A Logos Mysticism

At Goleta, California, in the Newman Chapel of the University of California at Santa Barbara, a unique, provocative mural dominates the wall behind the altar. The artist, Michael Dvortsak, basing his work on Teilhard de Chardin's belief that, since the Word became flesh and lived among us, "Christ invests Himself organically with the very majesty of His universe," has sought to draw out in dramatic, pictorial form the implications of the Incarnation in language that students studying at a modern university would understand.

Christ is depicted with arms outstretched, in a crucified form. In a circular movement pouring down from one hand and up to the other are the vivid symbols of a living world, that of the inner space of the submicroscopic and that of outer space, of the macrocosm, of planets and galaxies and quasars.

Christ looks down with intense interest and spiritual concern towards every created atom. The artist stresses the unity of the whole created universe in Christ, who has taken on matter and is "inside" the universe, creating, developing, and divinizing it until all is brought back in glory to the Father. It is an artistic profession of the faith proclaimed by St. Paul: "...for in Him were created all things in heaven and on earth, everything visible and everything invisible" (Col. 1,16).

The whole life cycle is shown to come forth from Christ, through Him and in Him, starting with the individual unicell of life, to the union of sperm and ovum, to the formation of the foetus. From the mountains and valleys making up man's complicated inner, physical world, to the planets and galaxies of outer space, all things sweep out and down in the shape of a human heart from the head of Christ, back up from the bottom through the figure of Christ.

The artist is showing us that God loves His creation. The world is full of vibrant energy, God's own concerned, loving activity through the Incarnate Word. The Body of Christ is being formed by the matter of this universe as each atom is brought by man the contemplator under the power of Christ. God loves the world that is of His making. It is good, and He is involved in its future. He is present in it as an inner force, making it evolve; He lives for it, dies for it. There is hope for this wildly careening universe, because there is a principle of harmony at its center. This principle is Christ the Evolver, Christ the *Logos.*

AN ORDERED LOVE

The Trinity, absolute inaccessibility, self-contained in its inner perfection, still seeks, as part of this perfection, to pour itself out in order that its Goodness may be shared. The "otherness" of the created world, its "worldliness," insofar as it is not God, is ultimately its whole scope of existence. Because we are created distinct from God, in His love for us and in His desire to share His life with us, we possess the possibility of growth. And growth means life and love.

Christ is the Word, the Logos, through whom God speaks to us, and in that Speech we have our being. The abyss between God and nothingness is spanned through the Logos. He is man's *raison d'être,* the reason why man is, and why the whole world was created and given into the mighty hands of man to make his awesome response to the Giver of life. Man cannot be united to God in order to reach his fulfillment unless God gives Himself to man. "God's love for us was revealed when God sent into the world His only Son so that we could have life through Him" (I Jn. 4,9). St. Paul clearly shows us the plan of God's creation: "We are God's work of art, created in Christ Jesus to live the good life as from the beginning He had meant us to live it" (Ephes. 2,10).

When God's Logos assumed flesh, our humanity, when He took upon Himself matter, as eternally ordained by God in the total plan of creation, man and the whole material world were irrevocably assumed into that hypostatic union. As divinity and humanity were joined into one being "without confusion," as the Council of Chalcedon (A.D. 451) described the hypostatic union, so by analogy man and the world are joined together with divinity without confusion but in a unity of love. As the human nature of Christ, living united with His divinity for all eternity, will always remain His glorified humanity, so too this created world will come into its fullness precisely by entering into a conscious relationship of love with God. Christ is acting within the evolving process of this world to allow the world to be itself and to let man become his true self.

Regardless of whatever culturally conditioned theological or philosophical vehicle they employed in interpreting the Christian message, the mystics, universally and throughout the centuries of Christianity, have moved within the context of a dynamic and evolutionary process of the unfolding of the God-man-world relationship.

As the mystic is led progressively into the inner meaning of reality, he is not led away from the created world, but rather he is led into reverence and worship of God as present everywhere within the created world. The flowers, the trees, birds, animals, the beauties of each new season, the sun, moon, stars, the mountains, lakes, oceans: the whole world reveals to the contemplative the loving presence of God, concerned to give Himself to man in His many gifts. God is contemplated as an almighty Transcendence that is the Source of all created life.

The mystic moves even deeper into reality when he adores the presence of God as the One who "contains" the created world, gives it its "consistency." As Paul preached to the Athenians, our God ". . .is not far from any of us, since it is in Him that we live and move and exist. . ." (Acts 17,28). Man is not alone; God is everywhere, present and holding up all of existence.

The mystic breathes and realizes in his breath and in the breath infused into every living being that it is the uncreated energies of God which give man and his world the capacity to evolve into children of God. Creation for the mystic is an on-going process. Whatever is, is a point of meeting God the Doer, the almighty Force energizing the universe. Above all, man finds within Himself a special share in God's energies in his power to know personally God and to love and surrender himself to Him. Thus the mystic can no longer be content with merely adoring the beautiful, harmonious presence of God in His universe. The mystic surrenders his energies to those of God. A new communion of love is reached as man seeks to "do" with

God according to God's plan. Man's impulsiveness now changes to utter receptivity in his openness to cooperate with the energies (graces) of God operating at each moment in each event.

The mystic's response to this presence of God acting in all creatures is to return love by man's loving activities. Man submits his whole being, especially his intellectual and volitional powers, to God, in order to become, in the words of St. Paul, "re-concilers" with Jesus Christ of the whole universe back to the Father. Above all, the mystic pierces through the illusion of values that pamper the senses, that exalt the independence of a self-centered existence, in order to arrive at a faith-vision that actively allows man to "suffer" with God suffering in the world. The mystic sees God's loving hand in the "pruning" of the vine branch in order to bring forth more fruit. By total death to self there is effected gradually a more perfect union with God in more perfect love. Rather than running away from the world, the mystic is now totally at God's disposition to work according to God's will, in order to bring the world into its greater spiritual existence, into greater unity of love.

Teilhard de Chardin has aptly expressed the mysticism of activity propelled by a vision of God's active love for man:

> To adore formerly meant preferring God to things, by referring them back to Him and sacrificing them for Him. To adore now has come to mean pledging oneself body and soul to creative act, by associating oneself with it so as to bring the world to its fulfillment by effort and research. Loving one's neighbor formerly meant not defrauding him and binding up his wounds. Charity, from now on, while not ceasing to be imbued with compassion, will find its fulfillment in a life given

for common advance. Being pure formerly meant, in the main, standing aside and preserving oneself from stain. Tomorrow chastity will call, above all, for a sublimation of powers of flesh and of all passion. Being detached formerly meant not concerning oneself with things and only taking from them the least possible. Being detached now means step-by-step moving beyond all truth and beauty by power of very love that one bears for them. Being resigned, formerly could signify passive acceptance of present conditions of the universe. Being resigned now will be no longer allowed, save to the warrior fainting away in the arms of the angel.[1]

Far from being an easy mysticism, encouraging a sickening quietism, such a vision of prayer is at the heart of the Christian message of the cross leading to the resurrection. There is a transformation of the universe to the degree that man, the cooperator with God's activity, dies to his own views and values and submits in loving surrender to the inner power of God's Spirit revealing the plan of harmony. This vision of the contemplative life will always stand as the essential characteristic separating a Logos mysticism from all other forms of mysticism.

A PATRISTIC VISION

The Eastern Fathers theologized from their lived, mystical experiences. Filled with the Holy Spirit, they could equally move from a study of man, of the events in all creation, to the study of Holy Scripture through various levels of God's revealing presence and loving activity. The ordinary man in the West tends to view the unfolding of his life through the three spatial dimensions of length, breadth, and depth, and the temporal dimensions of past, present, and future. The space-time continuum is the context in which our human actions unfold in succession; we divide our whole lifetime, our whole movement from the beginning progressing to the end in space-time categories. All too often our relationship to God is similarly expressed and lived in these terms.

But the truth that God is love and life, that He is known as a *total* experience in a prayerful life, soon becomes reduced to the concept of a God before creation, a God in creation and a God after creation. Gradually, God becomes quite impersonal, while our response, instead of being addressed to God as a person in love, comes to be measured by these categories of space and time and often, unfortunately, only by extrinsic rules or moral laws of conduct.

The Eastern Fathers, because they were mystics, had the ability of viewing the history of salvation from the unified perspective of God. They could transplant themselves to a higher vantage point and could view the continuity of events from the Old Testament to the New Testament to our own day in the light of the all-encompassing present moment, the *now* of God. Though they knew they were situated in the time that unfolded after the historical Person, the Logos Incarnate, had already come to earth, they also knew that they were in the present moment as regards God's love. They were dominated by this eternal act of love that is always permanent, always constant, whether in the first moment of creating this universe or man or in developing man after the fall or in the first moment of the physical Incarnation of Christ or in the glorified life of the risen Christ now present, immersed immanently in this universe of ours.

The Fathers always saw the same God unfolding His eternal love for us in an area that is out of space and time, although it is unfolding within the historical categories of our space and time. I like to call this the *fourth* dimensional perspective of the early Fathers; they could see this Trinitarian activity ever operaring in history, bringing about His eternal plan as conceived according to His Word, the Divine Logos Whom the Father is eternally speaking and in Whom, through Whom and with Whom all things are being brought forth. This is the dynamic vision found in St. John's Gospel: the Logos operating in the universe to bring us the glory of God. This is St. Paul's vision of the whole world unfolding gradually into a new creation:

> And for anyone who is in Christ, there is a new creation; the old creation has gone, and now the new one is here. It is all God's work. It was God who reconciled us to Himself through Christ and gave us the work of handing on this reconciliation (2 Corin. 5:17-18).

THE LOGOS AND THE LOGOI

The Fathers' doctrine of the Logos evidently comes from the teaching of St. John's Gospel. Before John had formulated his doctrine of the Logos made flesh, the Greeks had various philosophical interpretations of the term, but fundamentally the logos meant "not only the side of God which is reflected in creation, which touches the finite world; it is the ultimate reason which explains all existence, the eternal principle that underlies phenomena."[2]

For Heraclitus, the Logos is the eternal principle that gives continuity and pattern to a universe that is always in change or flux. Philo the Alexandrian, a Jewish author, combined both the Hebrew and Hellenistic traditions and in addition identified the Logos with the Ideal Man, i.e., man as conceived in the mind of God.

In the Sapiential Books of the Old Testament, the Logos was the creating Word of God by which He "spoke, and they were made, He gave His command, and their frame was fashioned" (Ps. 32,9).

But John's Gospel gives a totally new revelation of Logos theology. For John, the Logos is the very principle of all that is and all that lives. It is found in each created thing and yet it is distinct from the creature. This principle hides within the depths of God. This is Yahweh's *Debar* that He eternally speaks. It lies within God from eternity and is itself God.

> In the beginning was the Word;
> the Word was with God
> and the Word was God.
> He was with God in the beginning.
> Through Him all things came to be,
> not one thing had its being but through Him.
> All that came to be had life in Him
> and that life was the light of men...
> The Word was the true light
> that enlightens all men;
> ...The Word was made flesh,
> He lived among us,
> and we saw His glory,
> the glory that is His as the only Son of the Father,
> full of grace and truth (Jn. 1:1-14).

This Logos, God, Life, Light, becomes man like us, identifies with us in order that He may lead us out of darkness into the true Light, into His very being, that is one with the glory, the *Shekinah*, of the awesome Godhead. This pre-existent Word of God, God Himself, is the meaning of the universe that existed before it was created; He becomes the model, the pattern by which the

world is made; He is also the *power* that generates the
world into being, especially the power that begets man
into his fullness as sharers of His own glory, that of His
Father, by making us children of the same Father.

MAXIMUS THE CONFESSOR: A LOGOS MYSTIC

Of all the Church Fathers, Maximus (+662) gives us
the most complete vision of a Logos mysticism, sum-
marizing and perfecting all that Origen, Athanasius and his
other predecessors had written on this point. For Maximus as for St. John, the whole world is inter-related in its
harmony according to the differentiated *logoi* or the
created existences of individual things according to the
mind of God. All things are created through the Logos
through whom the creative will of the Father flows.
Irenaeus had said that the two hands of God bringing forth
the universe were Jesus Christ and the Holy Spirit. But
with Maximus, most of the other Fathers were not too
concerned to highlight the creative power of the Spirit in
preference to the central role of the Logos in giving
creation its full meaning.

The *logos* in each being is the principle of existence
which relates a given creature to God as its Cause; it also
denotes the created existence of a thing founded in God's
will that it should have existence. It is the principle of a
coming-to-be and implies a participation in God as being.
These *logoi* pre-exist in God and are contained in the
Logos, the Second Person of the Trinity who is the first
principle and final end of all created things.[3]

It should be noted, as Polycarp Sherwood points out,
that these logoi in the mind of God are not "inert models
but the very creative power of God, realizing itself in the
creature."[4]

Hence we see a very dynamic vision of a world united in the mind of God, of a world of ideal *logoi* in process of being attained as the existential *logoi* in creatures move to completion under the power of the Logos, Jesus Christ. Inanimate objects have to exist according to their God-given *logoi;* they have no choice. But it is man who is the center of this whole universe. He possesses free will—the ability to live according to the *logos* in him, by fulfilling, in union with God's activity (energy-grace), this inner principle of harmony and order; or else he could reject it.

For Maximus, the truly *real* man is he who lives according to the logos, and this logos is modeled on a conscious relationship in loving submission to the Logos living within man and bringing forth his potencies to be a child of God. Christ is the perfect Logos, the full image who most perfectly reflects the mind of God. We have our total being insofar as we have a loving relationship to Christ, allowing Him to fulfill within us that image destined to be brought to perfection in our first creation by the potency God has given us. This image or logos is to be actuated by a lifetime of knowledge and virtue. The unnatural man does not live according to his logos but according to the principle of the *Alogos,* the Evil One, whose principle is not self-sacrificing love but rather *philautia* or self-love.

For Maximus the great force which accomplishes self-mastery, detachment, and harmonization of man's faculties according to his nature is *love.* "Love, the divine gift, perfects human nature until it makes it appear in unity and identity by grace with the divine nature," says Maximus.[5]

Charity is not only the highest virtue; it is the reality which embraces all, the link with the world of grace; it is the force that unites those that are differentiated. It brings about the union of the Word and human nature, the union of the personal energies which egoism, self-love, has dispersed; it effects union between all men.[6]

In Maximus' thought, this growth in charity and progress in the ascetic life are two aspects of a single process: the purification of the passions and their subsequent conversion in the ascetic life are brought about by charity. The same vital force of desire or love, expended in the gross passions, is sublimated and turned to God. Maximus writes:

> For him whose mind is continually with God, even his concupiscence is increased above measure into a divinely burning love; and the entire irascible element is changed into divine charity.[7]

GROWTH IN CONTEMPLATION

The Greek Fathers, as typified by Maximus, conceived man's growth in contemplation as a synergism, a cooperation under the power of God's energies, called grace, whereby man does all he can to purify his "heart" from all self-centered love, thus to open himself up to God's more personal communication in contemplation. Hence there are not three steps, the purgative, illuminative, and unitive ways. There is *praxis, vita practica,* in which man builds up virtue, modeled on the human life and teaching of Jesus Christ, and destroys all vices impeding the presence of God from completing His divinization of man. Man never leaves this "practical life;" he is always in need of *nepsis* (sober vigilance) and *prosochi* (attention) to control his inner thoughts from which flow either inordinate desires and actions or a state of "passionate indifference" or *apatheia*, where all of man's irascible and concupiscible passions are submitted to the will of God, spoken through the sensitivity of a purified heart turned ever upon the inner Logos dwelling within man.

The next stage Maximus calls *theoria physica*. It is the beginning of God's infusion of contemplation whereby man can contemplate the inner *logoi* within all creation. In created things, Sacred Scripture and man himself, the contemplative is able to move beyond the surface that presents itself to the senses to arrive at an inner knowledge given by God that relates the given creature to the mind of God. By knowing a thing in all its reality, the mystic intuitively sees its relationship to Jesus Christ. To quote again Teilhard's phrase that perfectly summarizes the goal of the *vita contemplativa*, the mystic begins to see "Jesus Christ shining diaphanously through the whole world."

The highest stage of infused contemplation, *theoria theologica*, or simply called by Maximus *theologia*, is where the most intense degree of "deification" takes place. God no longer reveals Himself through the *logoi* in creatures, but the Trinitarian life unfolds within the soul of the mystic. A union of man's humanity with God's divinity takes place similar to the *perichoresis*, the assimilation of two natures in the hypostatic union, human and divine. God reveals Himself in Maximus' apophatic theology now through no concepts derived from the created world but rather only through an immediate awareness given to man of God's holy and loving presence.[8] In that awareness by experiential knowledge, man becomes through divinization *(theosis)*, through a participation in grace, what Jesus Christ was by nature. God is no longer an object to man. A union now of perfect inner communication and interpenetration takes place. Man enters into

God. Although man still exists as a human being, yet he knows now a new mode of existence. Two wills in love are virtually one.

MAN–THE COSMIC MEDIATOR

Maximus conceives man's role through higher contemplation as effecting the unity of God's plan; he becomes a "reconciler" of a world that is brought into being already divided in its inner being. Keeping in mind the above three stages of prayer, we can gain some keen insights into the mystic's cosmic relations by examining Maximus' five divisions that contemplation of the higher degrees brings together into a harmony and unity. In *Ambigua 41* we find the first of these rifts in nature as the division between the sexes. He sees this division as existing on the physical level as well as on the psychic level, in the analogical division between the "male" which represents anger (of the irascible passions) in the individual and the "female" which represents concupiscence. He is more interested in the psychological union that will transform the elements of anger and concupiscence. This is attained primarily in the *praxis* stage.

The second division is between Paradise and the inhabited earth. This is cultivated by a life of virtues with Christ as man's model. The way to Paradise has been reopened by Christ through His death and His life of virtues. Hence now through man's obedience to His commandments and inspirations, man imitates Christ and leads a "godlike way of life."[9]

The third division, that between heaven and earth, is mediated by man through his proper contemplation of all sensible creation. Man is thus able to see the "within" of things, their *logoi.* In apprenhending these *logoi,* man recognizes that they are reducible to a common *logos* which unites them all in a common purpose established by God in creating them. In this recognition of a ground of unity for all earthly realities in their *logoi,* man ascends, as it were, with Christ to His Father in heaven and thereby overcomes the division between heaven and earth. This ascent of man in contemplation is his response to Christ's condescension to him in His Incarnation.

The fourth division, between intelligible and sensible creation, is overcome by man in a higher form of contemplation which reduces all *logoi* of sensible creation to one single principle, one *logos* of all creation. This common principle is Jesus Christ, the divine Logos which contains all creation. This experience prepares man for the highest degree of contemplation; Jesus, the Way, leads us to the Trinity itself.

The final division which the mystic is to overcome in order to bring the world into its fullness is that between God and creation. It is overcome only in mystical union, the state of pure prayer in which man "leaves" the sphere of creation by ecstasy and is united to God beyond his own nature. The principle and mode of this unity is above man's nature. It comes from the very love-grace of God. Man's highest work in this life is "to reunite by love created with uncreated nature, showing the two in unity and identity through the acquisition of grace." [10]

The sacraments open man to God's grace to effect this unity, first in man, then through his reconciling work in the universe. Especially Baptism and the Eucharist are the sacraments wherein the divinization power of Christ works most effectively in man. The Church is also a place of encounter with Christ's deifying grace. The Church is a microcosm of what will be accomplished by God's grace throughout the whole human race. Both now in the Church and then in the whole world all distinctions will remain and yet paradoxically will be annihilated. Maximus describes this synthetic union:

> Men, women and children profoundly divided as to race, nature, language, manner of life, work, knowledge, honor, fortune. . .the Church recreates all of them in the Spirit. To all she equally communicates a divine aspect. All receive from her a unique nature which cannot be broken asunder, a nature which no longer permits one henceforth to take into consideration the many and profound differences which are their lot. [11]

ROLE OF THE HOLY SPIRIT

St. Cyril of Jerusalem, who had developed a pastoral sacramentology, especially of Baptism and Confirmation, calls the Holy Spirit, the One who stamps the seal of Jesus Christ upon each Christian. "Do not forget the Holy Spirit at the time of your illumination. He is ready to stamp your soul with His seal." The word seal, *sphragis,* was most widely used in early Christianity as a sign of belonging to the one whose seal was stamped on the forehead of the slave or animal. The sealing by the Holy Spirit means that the Holy Spirit imprints onto us the Father's likeness, i.e., the Lord Jesus, according to whose image and likeness we have been created. From that moment we do not belong any more to ourselves.

Maximus likewise sees the operation of the Holy Spirit taking place especially in the sacraments and in unceasing prayer. In every phase of man's spiritual development into a greater likeness to Jesus Christ, the Spirit is active. For Maximus, the Holy Spirit is at work in

man's purification accomplished through fear, reverence
and knowledge. The Spirit illumines the *logoi* of things and
gives knowledge of the inner relationship of all things to
Christ. It is He who bestows perfection through simple
wisdom on those worthy of deification. [12]

The Holy Spirit, as conceived by all of the Greek
Fathers, is the agent who divinizes, the Sanctifier. By His
indwelling in man as in His temple, He makes the divine
life present in man grow continuously. His work is to
reveal and make present Jesus Christ, the Logos, within us
and in all of the world. The Spirit leads us to experience
God as Father, *Abba.* He brings the Trinity to man's
consciousness. Hence through the Spirit man is able to
pray unceasingly, according to the ideal of the early
Fathers of the desert and the ideal of all Christians.
Christians, as St. Jude exhorts us, must "use the most holy
faith as your foundation and build on that, *praying in the
Holy Spirit;* keep yourselves within the love of God and
wait for the mercy of our Lord Jesus Christ to give you
eternal life" (Jude, 20).

MYSTICS OF THE LOGOS

Today we are in contact with the religious classics
and with spiritual masters of other religions more ancient
than even Christianity. The same Spirit has been always
and still is today working in the hearts of all men, who
have without exception been made by God according to
the Image and Likeness of God that is Jesus Christ. This
Holy Spirit comes to us and forms, creates us into deiform,
divinized beings, permeated by the Divine Trinitarian
energies working and loving within us. But it is in and
through the Logos made flesh, Jesus Christ, that we have

the amazing assurance that our assimilation into the Godhead makes it possible that we enter into our true uniqueness, not by absorption, but by the love we experience in the Father through the Son in His Spirit and by the love we then have for each person and creature made by God in and through that Logos.

In every mysticism the experience of the Absolute becomes more unified, less diffused. The separation is of the false ego; the union takes place between the true *I* and its being in the Other who is ultimate and has no second. But the Spirit of Jesus makes it possible for the Christian mystic to become aware of himself, not as a subject, adoring a divine object, but as the *I* aware of itself as a child, a son of God, a divinized being participating, as St. Peter says, in the Divine Nature, but not losing its human nature, not becoming God by its nature, but nonetheless truly deified by God's loving presence within. The mystics became aware of this when they experienced God deep down as the core of their very being. In the depths of our being He is found as a Person, closer to ourselves than we to ourselves, penetrating us completely.

What mystic has not experienced in this assimilation that which Maximus and so many other mystics have described in their analogy of iron and fire?[13] The iron and fire are found together in a fiery sword, but the piece of iron effects exactly that which is in accordance with its own nature. It glows as fire, but in a way that is proper to iron. The glowing sword cuts and burns at the same time; as iron it cuts, as fire it burns. [14]

The Christian is given the fantastic privilege by faith of actually being immersed into the fire of the Logos both in deep, contemplative prayer and in the Eucharist which cannot really be separated as two distinct moments of loving adoration. Yet the Logos incarnated does not come to us alone. He is, by His essence as Logos, *relational.* He points to the Father, and He points from the Father to us. "I am in the Father and the Father in me" (Jn. 14, 10). Where Christ, the Divine Son, is, there also is the Father. "He that sent me is with Me and He has not left Me along...The Father abides in Me (Jn. 13, 29; 14, 10). Where the Father and Son are present, there also is the Holy Spirit, who loves the Father and the Son within us and with us. The three Persons do not remain inactive within the contemplative. Within, the Father utters His Word; He generates His Son, who is perfectly the Image of His Father, the Divinie Logos, by a perfect response of love which, with the love of the Father for the Son, breathes forth the Holy Spirit.

The Logos not only brings this Trinitarian union with us about by His presence, but by His activity within, He speaks to us of the Father. The Holy Spirit loves the Father and the Son within us and with us. Christ teaches me to realize His love as Logos for His Father. He teaches us about the Father and the Holy Spirit, but He also associates His activities as Son with our potency to respond likewise in union with Him to a similar act of sonship towards our Heavenly Father. He teaches us how to adore, praise, love, surrender ourselves of every element that is an obstacle to true Sonship in God by repeating within us; "Behold, I come to do Thy will." He asks the Father that we be admitted into the mystery of divine love. "Father, I pray for them also...that they may be one in us" (Jn. 17, 20). He demands of the Father and obtains our participation in His filial surrender of self to the Father. "Father, may the love wherewith you have loved me be in them" (Jn. 17, 26).

But as the mystic of the Logos goes out into the world of multiplied beings, He continues to speak to him of the Father's great love in every material creature that he contacts. DeCaussade's sacrament of the present moment becomes for him a reality as the Logos from within leads him to see the stamp of the Trinity on each creature, on each event of every moment.

In conclusion we end with the beinning: Jesus Christ, the Alpha and Omega, the Image of the Father according to whose Image we have been created in potency to be contemplatives of that Logos, to become "sons of God and coheirs of Heaven," as St. Paul said. Through a more intense, expanded consciousness of the transcendent presence of the Trinity, living and acting in all material creatures out of love for us, we too can enter into a more vivid act of faith in that Trinitarian Life living within us and loving us. The sense-phenomenal world will be a true symbol to such contemplatives; not only will it point out to us the hidden, acting presence of the Trinity, but also the material world will effect what it stands for. The material world will be the point of a personal encounter effecting a true union with a Father loving us as He loves His only begotten Son, with the Son loving His Father in union with us, the newly divinized sons of God, not by nature but by His uncreated energies, His grace, in union with the Holy Spirit, the bond of mutual love between the Father and His Son and His adopted sons.

7

"Weep—There Is No Other Way"

Although there will always be one Christian spirituality, that based on Christ's revelation and the imitation of His virtues, still the Eastern Christian tradition presents approaches, points of emphasis and accents different from those found in the Western tradition.

One central idea strongly stressed in the Christian East is that of purification and *penthos,* or compunction of heart. In the West when we speak about compunction, purification and the constant thought of our sins, we regard it as totally negative precisely because, I believe, we have lost the concept of our littleness of heart, the conviction of our absolute need for God's justice or His mercy, a conviction resulting from the realization of our true, ontological position in regard to God. It is evident throughout all the Eastern Fathers' writings that the first step in the spiritual life is always to put ourselves before God as we really are, which is in a state of nothingness. We are nothingness before Allness, and so it is only natural that we find that Christian spirituality is based on this polarity: the transcendence of God and man's own littleness. Strangely enough, far from breeding in us any sadness or longfaced remorse or introspection, the realization of our nothingness before God is what gives us true

Christian joy; indeed, it fills us with great, child-like confidence in God.

Some years ago I was able to spend two summers on Mount Athos where, after I had studied in Rome the spirituality of the Eastern Fathers, I wanted to visit the monks of Karoulia. Karoulia is the southernmost tip of Mount Athos where a small group, about thirty monks, still live in little hermitages or huts and practice the ancient and strict form of *hesychasm.* Fundamentally, this hesychasm is the key Byzantine spirituality of the Eastern Fathers, beginning with the Fathers of the Desert. Gradually through the centuries this developed into a physical method of prayer. But the physical part of the method is actually, I believe, the result of an influence of Moselm mysticism which ultimately comes from Hindu and Buddhist mysticism. In Moslem practice, the penitent tries, by focusing all his attention on one part of his body or upon an object and by repeating a *dhikr* or sacred name or word, to synchronize his breathing with the spiritual movements of his soul.[1] Gradually he moves into that interior depth of his being where he finds the core or center of his existence and he unites himself there with God. This method is not essential to true hesychasm.

One of the basic points in the formulation of Byzantine hesychasm was precisely this concept of compunction which the Greek Fathers called *penthos.* Arsenius, one of the early monks who left the Byzantine court to flee into the desert, had heard a voice telling him to *"fuge, tace et quiesce,"* "flee, keep silent and be at rest." These three injunctions have more or less been the core of the hesychastic spirituality. They demand a fleeing, a withdrawal from the spirit of the world, and a silence, at least an interior silence of the heart. The *quies* is the necessary tranquillity wherein the total being becomes integrated, so that there is no more self-seeking dispersion of the passions in all directions. Everything is coordinated and under the influence of grace. The doctrine of weeping or having compunction for one's sins, known as *penthos,* forms one of the basic spiritual approaches to God among Eastern Christians.

At Karoulia on Mount Athos the thing that intrigued me most was to see whether this type of spirituality was viable for today, or whether it was merely a museum piece. Here I found the same asceticism that was practiced in the 3rd, 4th, and 5th centuries, when the Egyptian desert became a "thebaid" of monks, thousands of whom fled the pagan world so that they could take the Gospel literally in all its stark simplicity. I had found on every page of the writings of the Fathers, in the *Apophthegmata Patrum,* in the *Life of St. Anthony* written by St. Athanasius, in Macarius' homilies, in the writings of Evagrius of Pontus, John Climacus and Simeon the New Theologian, in the *Philokalia,* the special collection of hesychastic writings, always the same approach beginning with compunction of heart. On Mount Athos I found the same approach. It is really a lost concept in the West, and I do believe that we must go back to this concept, because this is truly the only way that we can ever preserve a true ontological relationship to God. We will, especially in America, always be tempted to bring God down to *our* level.

PENTHOS LEADS TO TRUE ENLIGHTENMENT

In our thirst for democracy we find it very difficult to appreciate a reverential awe in the presence of God. In our pragmatism, in our up-and-doing drive, we show ourselves to be fundamentally Pelagians. We concentrate on what *we* must do and we never really let God take over in our lives. The reason is, precisely, that we have forgotten our own ontological nothingness. *Penthos* gives us, I think, a permanent environment wherein a true relationship with God is maintained. This is the only way that God will really come down and reveal Himself to us. All that we can learn on our own about God is really nothing or so very little, but when God reveals Himself to us, and He does this only to the meek and humble of heart, then we can make genuine progress in the spiritual life. But there must be first of all this littleness brought about by a spiritual weeping for sins. Abbot Pimen, one of the early Egyptian Fathers, expressed their common thinking: "Weep for your sins, there is no other way to salvation." They were completely convinced that this weeping kept them from sinning and that this was the only way to true salvation, to true life, whereby God, even in this life, would come and dwell within them.

We in the West know about the purgative way, but for us, it is usually only at stated times in our retreats or in the Liturgy that we try to put on this mentality of sorrow for our sins; it is not an abiding "atmosphere" because we usually forget our true relationship to God. This is what we must recover; not introspection into our sinful past, by any means, nor scruples, but we must try to understand ontologically who we are before God. When we understand especially that we are sons and daughters of God through God's merciful love and that we have in the past turned away from God, that we were temples of God and we desecrated these temples, then we children can weep for the slightest offense against such a good and Heavenly Father.

It is a weeping, not necessarily physical, but rather an interior weeping upon seeing the goodness of God shining so strongly within us. The slightest turning away from God as from our only end fills us with great fear, a filial, reverential fear. The third beatitude reads: "Blessed are they who mourn, for they shall be comforted." It is sung often in the Byzantine Liturgy. It is precisely those who weep that will be comforted by God. God will come into such a soul and fill that soul with true happiness. And so the early Fathers, beginning with Origen, and then Ephrem, the Cappadocian Fathers Basil, Gregory Nazianzen and Gregory of Nyssa, John Chrysostom, and so on, all maintained this central doctrine of *penthos,* an abiding sorrow for our sins, compunction, as essential to any spirituality. St. John Chrysostom, in a homily on St. Matthew's Gospel, tells us of the necessity for every Christian to practice this compunction of heart.[2] He stresses, as does the author of the *Imitation of Christ,* that it is not necessary to be able to define compunction or to speak about it, but one must experience it in his own life He speaks of grief for past committed sins and, above all, for the possible loss of salvation, weeping at the sight of our own littleness and the fact that we might depend too much on our own powers rather than on the mercy of God. David is the model proposed in the Old Testament of this interior weeping. His attitude was not that of a slave towards a master but that of a child towards a Father who forgives in love.

METANOIA–CONVERSION

The early Fathers of the Desert felt that this dispostion was absolutely necessary. The words of Joel were repeated constantly, and we find this same sentiment

in the Byzantine Liturgy: "Be converted to me with all
your heart in fasting and in weeping and in mourning, rend
your hearts and not your garments, for merciful and
gracious is the Lord and ready to repent of evil." God will
never forgive our evils unless He sees in us a turning,
metanoia, a turning of the *nous,* the mind, back to God.
This is truly the attitude we should have in every Liturgy,
in every prayer to God. There must be always a conversion, a turning to God. Every day of our lives should be a
going to God. It is precisely this, I believe, that determines
the depth of our true conversion by making it grow deeper
and deeper.

So, we find the early Fathers feeding their disciples
with thoughts that would foster this true compunction,
that would remove any self-reliance, any Pelagianism, any
self-love. When we replace God by ourselves, our own little
puny powers, then truly God will not listen to our prayers.
He will have nothing to do with the hard of heart. This
doctrine of *penthos,* therefore, is certainly not a spiritual
delicacy for dilettantes. It is the "hard bread of athletes,"
as St. Paul says. It is not a fanciful thing that one reads
about, but it is something one has to experience throughout all his life in deep faith. We strive to realize that God
has forgiven us our sins in knowing that we are truly sorry,
and our sorrow is more perfect to the degree that we
understand not only our nothingness, but, and this is the
important thing, the allness of God, His goodness, His
mercy, His loveableness.

The Fathers of the Desert constantly tell us to think
about death. I remember once spending the evening with
two Greek monks on Mount Athos. These two monks lived
a communal life in a *skete* or small hermitage. Each
evening about 7:30 the two of them would go into the

chapel and would begin reciting the Jesus prayer: "Lord Jesus Christ, Son of God (the majesty of Christ, His goodness in becoming man), have mercy on me, a sinner (compunction, humility)." They started out quietly reciting this together, then they would break off and pray until midnight in silence. The Divine Liturgy was then celebrated at the end of which the celebrant, Father Ephrem, incensed a skull found on a table before the iconostasis. When I asked him later whose skull that was he simply answered that that was his spiritual guide, Father Joseph. There did not seem to be anything gruesome for Ephrem in this action nor in the mere fact that each day he gazed on the skull of his former spiritual guide. This was the most normal thing. He was a hard-headed realist, facing a fact from which he would not run away. Man is truly nothing, God is everything. He is the master of man's life and He will take it when He wants to do so. Yet the thing that amazed me in my short contact with Ephrem was that he impressed me as one of the happiest men that I had ever met. He radiated an interior peace and joy because there was nothing that he feared. He was truly a son of God and he knew it.

What does it mean to be a Christian? Are we really convinced of this tremendous truth that God is living in our souls? We will never be penetrated by this basic Christian truth until we understand who we are. We will never understand our relationship to God unless we arrive at this knowledge by means of this concept of *penthos,* compunction for our sins, the realization of our own ittleness and the possibility of going against God in the future.

One of the great doctrines in the East concerns an ffshoot of compunction, the constant yearning for tears, the gift of tears. Today no one writes in spiritual books about the gift of tears, and yet these Fathers of the Desert constantly exhorted their disciples to pray, beg God, cry out constantly day and night for the gift of tears. As Evagrius of Pontus says: "Before all else, pray to be given tears, that weeping may soften the savage hardness which is in your soul, and, having acknowledged your sin unto the Lord (Psalm 31), you may receive from Him the remission of sins."[3] It is true this is a mystical gift that God gives. It is not absolutely necessary, but the Fathers felt that when the soul was softened by years of this interior weeping, God would give this mystical experience. We find this same gift in the life of many Western saints, too. We think of St. Ignatius of Loyola, as he himself writes in his diary, how he would weep to such an extent that he could not read his breviary. All he had to do was to see the word "God" or "Jesus" and he would start weeping because of the tremendous interior illumination of his own nothingness which he received from God.

GOD'S GIFT

So, spiritual weeping is a gift from God. We do not receive it as a reward of our effort, but such a mystical gift usually follows progressively the degree of self-purification. We in the West judge all this to be very negative and certainly gruesome—constantly thinking about death and sin and sorrow and so on. Yet it is a basic principle among all the Eastern Fathers that the shadows of dark sorrow mingle with the light of God's illunination. It is there in sorrow that we find true joy—spiritual joy. Is it any wonder that the Eastern Fathers, in composing the Eastern Liturgy, settled on the litanies, answered by the *Kyrie*

Eleison, as the most perfect prayer? Why? Because they had such an intuition of the transcendence of God and man's own littleness that man could say nothing better than to repeat the prayer of the publican as he stood in the back of the synagogue, afraid to lift up his eyes. Standing there, he could only repeat while he struck his breast, "Lord have mercy on me, a sinner."

I think, therefore, that in our modern age we can find in this doctrine of compunction and abiding sorrow for sin certainly a dominant theme both of the Old and New Testament. It is precisely from Holy Scripture that the early Fathers developed this theme, in their hours of singing the psalter and feeding their minds on the Old and New Testaments. The Liturgy flows from Scripture, and thus we find likewise in the composition of the Liturgies this same emphasis on the reverence for and worship of God's majesty together with the sense of our own littleness and complete dependence on Him.

EFFECTS OF COMPUNCTION

The greatest effect of compunction highlighted by the fathers is the peace and joy that come through an experienced love of God toward the sinful individual. We can appreciate this even if we have not all experienced it to the same degree as did those early great athletes of Christ. Purified of all inordinate, passionate desires, such monks knew a permanently abiding sense of tranquillity that begot interior happiness. It was not the absence of troubles through a blind resignation to God's providence, as found so often in Muslim asceticism; nor a philosophical stoicism that basically feeds an inflated ego with a desire to be above all relationships to the world around it by simply

ignoring the rest of the world. This joy was at the basis of
the Christian experience: *Per crucem ad lucem.* Compunction was the dying process and joy was the resurrection of
all one's powers into a new life that produced a hundred-
fold in peace and happiness. Christ ended his beatitudes
with the promise: "Rejoice and be glad, for a rich reward
awaits you in Heaven." But Heaven was a condition that
even in this life was enjoyed by those who mourned. The
strangest paradox proved itself in experience as these early
monks wept before God and God comforted them. Their
interior joy, as their interior sorrow, had to manifest itself
in the exterior countenance. A quotation from Athanasius'
Life of Antony tells us more about this joy than any
analysis could give us. Antony excelled in compunction; he
also was radiant with joy:

> And besides, his countenance had a great and wonderful grace.
> This gift also he had from the Savior. For if he were present in
> a great company of monks, and anyone who did not know him
> previously wished to see him, immediately coming forward he
> passed by the rest and hurried to Antony, as though attracted
> by his appearance. Yet neither in height nor breadth was he
> conspicuous above others, but in the serenity of his manner
> and the purity of his soul. For as his soul was free from
> disturbances, his outward appearance was calm; so from the
> joy of his soul he possessed a cheerful countenance, and from
> his bodily movement could be perceived the condition of his
> soul, as it is written: 'When the heart is merry, the counte-
> nance is cheerful, but when it is sorrowful it is cast down.'
> (Prov. 15. 13). . . Thus Antony was recognized; he was never
> disturbed for his soul was at peace; he was never downcast,
> for his mind was joyous.[4]

In a marvelous way experienced by all who seriously
maintained themselves in this abiding compunction, God
revealed himself to them, not in any conceptual knowledge

deduced through a reasoning process, but in a direct, experimental knowledge that flooded the soul with an illumination of God's majestic grandeur. The shadows of dark sorrow mingle with the light of God's transcendence; and the Christian is content with repeating the only prayer that seems proper to the experience: "Lord, Jesus Christ, Son of God, have mercy on me, a sinner."

IN DEFENSE OF THOSE WHO WEEP

Paul J. Tillich in a short essay entitled "The Eternal Now" shows how repentance is more than a feeling of sorrow about wrong actions. "It is the act of the whole person in which he separates himself from elements of his being, discarding them into the past as something that no longer has any power over the present."[5]

Compunction, for the early Fathers of the desert and for all Christians who have grasped their insights, is the means the Christian uses to live in the "eternal now" while living also in a past, present, future continuum. God, for the fathers who wept "because there was no other way to perfection,"[6] was not a goal, an object toward which they moved and which they attained only upon death. God is the abundance of love that is ever overflowing in his uncreated energies and that inundates his creatures at every moment. Man, made to his image and drawn to the intimate relationship of a loving son to a loving Father, not only in the past has freely turned himself from greater growth by sin, but in the present and in the future feels the pull within and all around him of a world that is "groaning in travail" (Rom. 8. 22) until it reaches its perfection in Christ. This "existential *Angst*" cries for Another, One who lies beyond the ravages of time and space, One who is the possession of all perfections.

But it is compunction, that abiding sorrow for the godless past and the fear of a future without God, that allows man to contact God. God gives Himself to the weak, the poor, the needy; in a word, to the humble because they have entered into an experiential knowledge of their creaturehood. The desert fathers, crying incessantly with penitent David, *"Amplius lava me, Domine,* cleanse me fully, O Lord," experienced a second baptism. Climacus writes, "But sins committed after baptism are washed away by tears."[7] In this freedom from the past and the guilt that the future brings to him the Christian of true compunction gazes more clearly on the beauty and goodness of God. Filled with great tenderness and longing for greater union with God, the Christian finds his strength in his weakness. Because God has given him an abiding experience of his existential weakness, the Christian is filled with great tranquility and joy, since his strength is now in the all-powerful Father whose power he experiences mostly in God's tender forgiveness of man's weaknesses.

Instead of becoming introverted, the repentant Christian has a greater consciousness of his union with all nature in its need for the cosmic redemption of God's condescending love. Charity and tenderness are extended to all, for who cannot now understand the need to love and aid his fellow creatures when he himself witnesses constantly the love and aid of God toward himself?

Much is outdated and requires demythologizing in the writings of these fiercely serious Christians of an earlier age. But one truth will always remain the same, both for the monk in the Scete of Egypt of the fourth century and for the Christian of the cybernetic society of the twentieth century. We all have need of the Baptism of Christ, received not once, but over and over, whereby we are washed more and more of our own deep traces of resistance to God's love. But we receive the saving waters of Baptism only if we cry out constantly. We are in continual need of God's recreating force in our lives. And yet God is always the forgiving Lover, ready to burst into our meaningless flow of consciousness in time with his meaningful presence that allows us to make of *now* the eternal *Now* of God.

8

Transfiguration

The feast of the Lord's Transfiguration (August 6) is one of the major feasts celebrated among Eastern Christians. Usually on that day the faithful bring to the church fruit to be blessed and to be offered to God. This is the first fruit before the full harvest. Thus Christians manifest their thanksgiving to God for His protective love during the growing period of spring and summer and beg Him for a full harvest.

But there is a deeper faith-vision that penetrates this simple ritual. In this celebration Eastern Christians profess their faith in the total life-process as they experientally act out the mystery of the seed falling into the earth, later to bring forth fruit a hundredfold. Each Christian in Baptism becomes a seed implanted into the Church. There he is to grow to full maturity as a child of God. A *transfiguring* process is taking place over the spring, summer and autumn years of the Christian's life.

The Christian, endowed with the power of the Trinitarian life embedded into his being in Baptism, is being driven by God's inner activity and man's cooperation towards the fullness destined for him in Christ Jesus. The Christian's growth is a movement in assimilating love that divinizes as it both unites and distinguishes man in his uniqueness because of his consciousness that God loves him uniquely.

The feast of the Transfiguration celebrates the glorification of Jesus Christ of Nazareth. The Christians gather in faith to profess their belief that what was sown in ignominy was harvested in glory. Jesus Christ possessed a

> . . . . .state (that) was divine,
> yet He did not cling
> to His equality with God
> but emptied Himself
> to assume the condition of a slave,
> and became as men are;
> and being as all men are,
> He was humbler yet,
> even to accepting death,
> death on a cross.
> But God raised Him high
> and gave Him the name
> which is above all other names
> so that all beings
> in the heavens, on earth and in the underworld,
> should bend the knee at the name of Jesus
> and that every tongue should acclaim
> Jesus Christ as Lord,
> to the glory of God the Father (Phil. 2:6–11).

The Jews had killed Jesus the Nazarene, as Peter preached on the Pentecost, "but God raised Him to life" (Act 2, 24). "God raised this man Jesus to life and all of us are witnesses to that. Now raised to the heights by God's right hand, He has received from the Father the Holy Spirit. . ." (Acts 2:32–33).

Thus radiant joy transfuses this feast as Christians, looking at the beautifully colored fruits blessed on the table before the iconostasis, profess that "for us, our homeland is in Heaven and from Heaven comes the Savior we are waiting for, the Lord Jesus Christ and He will *transfigure* these wretched bodies of ours into copies of His glorious body. He will do that by the same power with which He can subdue the whole universe" (Phil. 3:20–21).

There is also a profession of faith on a cosmic dimension. The Transfiguration recalls St. Paul's vision of a world that is sown in corruption, that groans in travail, but that will rise and be transfigured into incorruptibility. Paul sees the risen Lord inserted as leaven in a batch of dough. He is drawing the whole universe into the fullness destined for it by His Father's eternal plan. Christ is already the absolute, universal head of the whole universe. He is recapitulating, bringing to completion, not only human beings made to His image and likeness, but the whole sub-human cosmos, which is to be brought into His person as He adores His Heavenly Father by returning the universe that was sown as a seed and is now fulfilled, ". . .that He would bring everything together under Christ as head, everything in the heavens and everything on earth" (Ephes. 1, 10).

God, the Source of all existence, "has put all things under His feet and made Him as the ruler of everything, the head of the Church which is His Body, the fullness of Him who fills the whole creation" (Eph. 1:22–23).

GOD'S BREATH IN MAN

What the Eastern Christian professes on the feast of the Transfiguration, the Christian mystic experiences over a long, gradual process of transfiguration into Christ. As he integrates the name of Jesus with his breathing, the physical breath is experienced no longer as separated from the very breath of God. The mystic begins to experience

God's dynamic presence within him as uncreated energies.

The story of Genesis becomes a living reality. "Then He breathed into his nostrils a breath of life and thus man became a living being" (Gen. 2, 7). God breathes His own very life into man. The contemplative, after years of deepening faith and continued purification, breaks through the dichotomy between God outside and man separated from Him. God's very life-giving breath is one with his breathing.

The "two hands of God," Jesus Christ and His Holy Spirit, to use St. Irenaeus' apt analogy, are continuously touching the soul, releasing new energies that are one with God's uncreated energies. These energies were there before, but now a *transfiguring* process has taken place. "There lives the dearest freshness deep down thing," as expressed so aptly in G. M. Hopkins' words from his *God's Grandeur.*

God touches the soul deeply, making His presence felt as a loving presence. The soul feels this searing presence penetrating its whole being, pulling it into a wholeness, a uniqueness that stretches forth as a prisoner out of steel-ribbed windows towards clear light in a hunger to be free. The mystic seeks only to surrender himself totally to the loving presence of God within. He suffers joyfully this action of God, creating, redeeming, transforming him into a greater oneness with Jesus Christ.

The overwhelming, unifying sentiment is, "My God, He loves me!" The soul feels loved, wanted, accepted, and this by Perfection itself! The communication of God to the soul and the soul's surrender of self to God admits of great degrees of intimacy and assimilation. Always the process brings one to a confusion of blurred lines. Where do I end and where does God begin? One really does not wait for the answer, because such knowledge has been superceded by a superior knowledge of experience that is content with the experience and fears that thoughts and words would destroy the sacredness of the adoring moment.

In such contemplation, the mystic of all true divine experiences "sees" and "feels" and "hears" and "touches" and "smells" and "tastes" the presence of God. The actions of sensations seem the only suitable analogy that renders the experience undergone by the mystic: God is directly and immediately being "sensed." He gives Himself in the most personalized act of self-giving. The contepla-tive can only compare the experience as "light from light '

The Byzantine mystics called it a participation in the Taboric *Light.* The light that transfused Jesus Christ along with Moses and Elias on Mount Tabor is experienced again within the human soul as a transfiguring power. Man experiences the fullness of his Baptism as he moves literally out of his existential darkness of self-centeredness into the light of God's Allness.

Nil Sorsky (+1508) who brought Byzantine hesy-chasm from Mt. Athos to Russia, writes in his *Ustav* or Rule:

> When the soul undergoes such spiritual activity and subjects itself to God and through direct union approaches the Divinity, it is enlightened in its movements by an intense light and the mind experiences a feeling of joy of the happiness that awaits us in the life to come. Then an indescribable sweetness warms the heart, the whole body feels its repercussions and man forgets not only any given passion, but even life itself and thinks that the Kingdom of Heaven consists of nothing other than this ecstatic state. Here he experiences that the love of God is sweeter than life and the knowledge of God sweeter than honey. . .[1]

But the classical description of the Taboric light has been given by Simeon the New Theologian:

> I see a light which is not of this world. Sitting in my cell, I see within me the Maker of the world; I converse with Him and love Him and I feed on this one Divine Image. Uniting with Him I am raised to the Heavens. Where is the body? I do not know, for God loves me and has received me into His very Being and hides me in His embrace and being in Heaven and at the same time in my heart. He becomes visible to me. The Ruler of all appears to me in a way equal to the angels, yet in a way more advantageous, for to them God is invisible and unapproachable while by me He is seen and He unites Himself with my being. It is this state that St. Paul described when he said that 'eye had not seen nor ear heard.' Being in this state, I do not have any desire to leave my cell, but I long to hide myself in a deep hole in the ground and there, removed from the upper world, I would gaze on my immortal Lord and Creator.[2]

ALL IS LOVED IN GOD

The touchstone that what a mystic is authentically experiencing is from God and not from his own imagination is found in the movement from within outwardly. We breathe inwardly and to that same degree we can breathe outwardly. The transfiguring power of God bathing the contemplative in His divinizing energy is also experienced by him in the world around him.

As the soul is immersed in God as the totally Other and finds its uniqueness in Him, so the soul opens itself to God in all creatures. The same powerful God that radiates His uncreated energies within us is found as the Source of being for all other creatures. The world around us takes on a new meaning. A transfiguring process is also taking place in our vision of the world and of ourself. We realize now that the world has not changed. Our vision has changed. God's presence was always there, but we were blinded to His light. Now it seems as though the blind have been given full sight. What lay in darkness before now is suffused with light. As we each see our uniqueness in God's love for us, so now we begin to experience the uniqueness of each creature in God's love for it. Yet what binds us even more now to God as our *allness* is the experience of Him as gift to us in His dynamic action in others.

G. M. Hopkins, S.J., called it "contuition," a simultaneous awareness of the individual concrete nature and of the dynamic presence of God there as the ground of its being. The contemplative simultaneously is aware of the created thing and intuitively sees its relationship to the creative eternal energies of God.

The Greek Fathers called this contemplation of material creatures *theoria physica,* the contemplation of the Logos in the created world. After purification we should move to a contemplation of the world around us. This world brings us to the inner world beyond the sensible, beyond the phenomenon. It is here that we really encounter the mind of God. Thus we move out of the realm of man's self-activity into the realm of God's influence. God gives us, by infusion, the gift to see, in all His creatures, the *logoi.* The *logos* of each creature is its principle of harmony that shows us the relationship of this creature to God's total providence, or to God's total order of salvation. Thus the whole world is interlocked and interrelated. Only he who has this gift of *theoria physica,* the contemplation of nature, can unlock that world and see the harmony existing among all these creatures, because he can see the purpose, the *raison d'être* behind every created being. Seeing that, naturally, he will act accordingly. He will never then misuse these creatures for his own purpose, but he must always use them and be used by them in the direct proportion that God intended them. So, this is the contemplation of the *logos* in each creature, and it is a wisdom given us by God that we could never deserve on our own. It comes to us purely from God, but in a way dependent upon our own purification. The purification of our souls prepares our whole being for this gratuitous infusion from God.

For the Eastern Fathers, to live fully according to nature is equivalent to living according to the *logos* within that given nature. The objects of true *physica theoria* or contemplation of creatures are not conceived in any philosophical sense. For Maximus the Confessor, the matter and form constituting a being's nature still make up the surface, the *superficies,* the *phenomenon,* the sensible. We can rightfully ask how one is to arrive at this understanding of the *logos* within creatures. Maximus the Confessor divides all created beings into three divisions: things, Sacred Scripture and man himself. In all of these three categories we find the *superficies,* the *epiphaneia,* that which presents itself to our senses. Then there is the inner knowledge of the *logos* or the principle of harmony giving the relationship of this or that created being to God's providence. This *logos,* as has been described above, is the reason of the creature's act of existence in the mind of God which corresponds to the wisdom of God in things. Persons without this infused gift from God of *physica theoria* or contemplation judge all things, Sacred Scripture and man himself by sense knowledge. But the person possessing this inner knowledge penetrates beyond sense knowledge of created natures, beyond the letter of Holy Scripture to the spirit or *pneuma;* he thus can see the real mind of God behind the written letter or beyond the exterior presentation of man to his inner mind or *nous* that gives us his real personality, his *logos*. The ordinary person reads Holy Scripture and sees nothing but the letter; he does not penetrate behind the type to the anti-type. Symbols in the Old Testament fail to reveal God's true mind, but the person with the gift of contemplation sees beyond the surface images. Every word, every picture tells him something deeper about God. The same applies to man in his relation with other men; a normal man views other men only as they present themselves to him externally. The man of interior vision can see beyond to the inner *logos;* he can pierce through the phenomenal, the physical appearance of the sensible order and enter into an interior vision that allows him to see that man in God's light.

The presence of God "must be instressed, stressed" in G. M. Hopkins' words. The contemplative sees in God's creative light through all of nature how each creature tumbles forth continually from God's loving involvement. He desires not to master and overpower nature, but rather, in an attitude of ever-increasing receptivity, he seeks not only to discover all things in God and God in all things, but he wishes to serve the Creator to render Him more adored and glorified by the entire universe.

Teilhard de Chardin said in his *Divine Milieu* that Jesus Christ was shining diaphanously throughout the whole world—for those who had eyes to see. As the contemplative advances in ever-deepening faith, he sees God everywhere as present and acting.

GOD—THE CENTER OF ALL BEING

God becomes the center of all other beings. This gives us a connatural affinity, a oneness with the world that

before, through our sinfulness, was threatened by our
aggressive power. St. Dorotheus, one of the early Fathers
of the desert, used the example of a wheel. The closer the
spokes move toward the center, the closer each spoke is to
each other. Evagrius insisted that he left men in order to
find them. The experience of all mystics is a new
knowledge and relationship to the world, a union in love
that begets in the mystic a burning desire to serve the
world.

As the contemplative intuits the created order as a
continued outpouring of the Trinity's love, God's gift to
him, he wishes to become, with St. Paul, a reconciler of
the whole universe through Christ back to the Father.

> And for anyone who is in Christ, there is a new creation; the
> old creation has gone, and now the new one is here. It is all
> God's work. It was God who reconciled us to Himself through
> Christ and gave us the work of handing on this reconciliation.
> In other words, God in Christ was reconciling the world to
> Himself, not holding men's faults against them, and He has
> entrusted to us the news that they are reconciled. So we are
> ambassadors for Christ; it is as though God were appealing
> through us, and the appeal that we make in Christ's name is:
> be reconciled to God (II Cor. 5:17-21).

A new creation is seen coming forth by the power of
Jesus Christ and His Spirit of love through man's adoring
cooperation. In Christ, God is incarnated and inserted into
the groaning universe. He sustains each creature in its
uniqueness and seeks to move each creature together with
the whole created universe into its *pleroma* or fullness.

The contemplative begins to experience the presence
of Christ everywhere, especially in other human beings.
Christ is laughing in the joyful; He is suffering in the
saddened. This oneness with Christ and the human scene is

best described by Caryll Houselander in her own "mystical" experience of Christ in a London subway:

> I was in an underground train, a crowded train in which all sorts of people jostled together, sitting and strap-hanging-workers of every description going home at the end of the day. Quite suddenly I saw with my mind, but as vividly as a wonderful picture, Christ in them all. But I saw more than that; not only was Christ in every one of them, living in them, dying in them, rejoicing in them, sorrowing in them—but because He was in them, and because they were here the whole world was here too, here in this underground train; not only the world as it was at that moment, not only all the people in all the countries of the world, but all those people who had lived in the past, and all those yet to come. I came out into the street, and walked for a long time in the crowds. It was the same here, on every side, in every passer-by, everywhere—Christ. . .
>
> The 'vision' lasted with that intensity for several days, and each of them revealed the mystery and its implications for me a little more clearly. Although it did not prevent me from ever sinning again, it showed me what sin is, especially those sins done in the name of 'love,' so often held to be 'harmless' for to sin with one whom you loved was to blaspheme Christ in that person, it was to spit on Him, perhaps to crucify Him. I saw too the reverence that everyone must have for a sinner; instead of condoning his sin, which is in reality his utmost sorrow, one must comfort Christ who is suffering in him. And this reverence must be paid even to those sinners whose souls seem to be dead, because it is Christ who is the life of the soul, who is dead in them; they are his tombs, and Christ in the tomb is potentially the risen Christ. For the same reason, no one of us who has fallen into mortal sin himself must ever lose hope.[3]

The contemplative has experienced himself growing into a greater, conscious relationship to Christ as image and likeness. He knows now on a deeper level that each human being has been made according to Christ, the Image of God. The more defaced is that image in man, the more ardently does the contemplative wish to re-create it, so that Jesus Christ again shines forth with all His divine splendor latent in each man. He wishes with great love and responsibility to serve his neighbor with an active love that will smooth away lines of fear and grief and consternation on the face of humanity. He rejoices too when Jesus Christ, the Eternal Youth, conquers man's heart in order to bring forth joy and happiness.

THE NAME OF JESUS POURED FORTH

God has taken a piece of this imperfect world and has transfigured it into His glorious, risen Son. "The end of the ages" has come upon us (1 Corin. 10, 11). It is the power, therefore, of the glorified Jesus, ever-present in this struggling world, that continues to transform creation into a new Jerusalem. Jesus, the high-priest, is still breathing over the groaning world to transfigure raw matter into a spirit-filled cosmos.

Yet Jesus Christ, as in history, needed the contemplative Mary to receive Him into her very being through the power of the Holy Spirit that hovered over her and then to be given as the Life to the world; so He needs other human beings to "beget" Him again, to render him "enfleshed" into a world that lies in darkness.

By our Baptism we are inserted into Him as co-sharers of His role as Prophet and Priest. St. Peter says, "But you are a chosen race, a royal priesthood, a consecrated nation, a people set apart to sing the praises of God who called you out of the darkness into His wonderful light" (1 Pet. 2, 9).

An ordained priest, celebrating the Divine Mystery according to the mind of Christ, breathes out the words of consecration over bread and wine, and Christians fall down to adore Jesus Christ, Son of God, gloriously reigning with the Father in Heaven and interceding for His children throughout the world. A baptized Christian utters the sacred Name of Jesus over a world that lies in darkness, and a redeeming light spreads over the horizon.

Although Jesus Christ, risen and glorified, is nowhere, since He can be confined in no place, yet He is everywhere because all times and places are under His eternal gaze; but He becomes still more present, in a loving, active way, when a human being, in loving adoration, calls His holy presence into a particular place and a particular time.

The English poet and martyr, Blessed Robert Southwell, S.J., once wrote: "Not where I breathe do I live, but where I love." Though Jesus Christ breathes His divinized breath throughout the whole cosmos, still when a contemplative utters His Name in love, He becomes present and alive in a new and marvelous way.

What a power the man of prayer possesses in the sacred Name of Jesus! He needs no cathedral, no choir, no vestments, no formal liturgies. He needs only faith to believe in the presence and power of Jesus. "The whole creation is eagerly waiting for God to reveal His sons" (Rom. 8, 19). Over the world of rocks and roses, fish and fowl, streams and oceans, valleys and mountains, the adorer calls forth the power of Jesus Lord to fulfill His creation.

Thus man returns to the Garden of Eden. The world of beast and bird is brought into harmony with God's purpose through the mediation of a worshipping, loving human being.

How much more can the contemplative bring human beings under the transfigured power of the risen Savior! A French novel, *Le Dieu a besoin des hommes,* well expresses the humility of God to make His redemptive love hinge upon the love of one man towards another, but then St. John tells us that if we love one another, it is because God lives in us, loving through us:

> No one has ever seen God;
> but as long as we love one another
> God will live in us
> and His love will be complete in us.
> We can know that we are living in Him
> and He is living in us
> because He lets us share His spirit.
> . . .God is love
> and anyone who lives in love lives in God,
> and God lives in him (1 Jn. 4, 12–16).

After His Ascension, Jesus Christ now lives in those who love Him. In His resurrection appearances, Jesus apparently assumed different forms in order to teach us that He cannot now be confined to one shape, one place, one time, one coming. Mary Magdalene looked at Him and saw a gardener; the disciples on the road to Emmaus saw a tired, hungry co-traveler; Peter and John and the disciples while fishing saw Him as a stranger on the shore preparing breakfast. Now He becomes a revealing and saving Lord in the outcast, the poor, the sick and suffering, the lonely, the imprisoned.

> For I was hungry and you gave me food; I was thirsty and you gave me drink; I was a stranger and you made me welcome; naked and you clothed me, sick and you visited me, in prison and you came to see me. Then the virtuous will say to Him in reply, 'Lord, when did we see you hungry and feed you; or

thirsty and give you drink? When did we see you a stranger
and make you welcome; naked and clothe you; sick or in
prison and go to see you?' And the King will answer, 'I tell
you solemnly, insofar as you did this to one of the least of
these brothers of mine, You did it to me, (Matt.25:35–40).

The true contemplative measures his degree of love
for Christ according to his desire to adore Him, surrender
himself totally to His Person and service to Him in His
creatures.

THE COMMUNION OF SAINTS

The transfiguring power of the contemplative is seen
in the Church's doctrine of the intercession of the Saints
and Angels. It is they who have attained the goal of
existence: to contemplate God. In this sense we can see
the reality of Purgatory as a form of therapy which
reconditions the spiritually retarded children of this world,
who, through lack of contemplation, were unaware of the
inner presence of the Trinity in all things during their
earthly-life. Leon Bloy wrote that the only tragedy at the
end of our lives is that we are not saints. We might say the
same for contemplation. If we have failed to advance in
contemplation during this life through God's grace, we
shall have to advance in the life to come through the
purifications called Purgatory.

But in this life, the Saints and Angels, so full of love
of God, immersed in His cosmic presence and desirous
only to adore and serve Him in the least of His creatures,
so that all things will be in God and God in all, need us
poor retarded children of God. Love needs to expand, to
continue to grow. Love that is static is death and no true
love. Love hungrily seeks to forget self and to give oneself
in creative suffering for the other.

This is a good definition of Jesus Christ, God incarnate. He is always surrendering Himself completely as the perfect, visible Image of the invisible God with the same eternally, unchangeable will-act of surrender that He made on the Cross. But we have no other way of experiencing this self-surrendering love of God for us except through the mediation of the sacrificing love others show toward us. The Angels and Saints, according to Catholic doctrine, are continually concerned for us mortal beings, striving to make us experience that for which Paul prayed, "All I want is to know Christ and the power of His resurrection and to share His sufferings by reproducing the pattern of His death" (Phil. 3, 10).

A COSMIC LITURGY

The mystic walks in communion with the Saints as present, and even more so by their purified love, than other earthly humans. He sees "inside" each creature to find God present there. His faith makes him vividly aware of this presence as he celebrates the Divine Liturgy, when, in microcosmic fashion, Jesus the High-Priest breathes over a small segment of the Church, including their gifts of bread and wine, and His Spirit of love transfigures this part of the incomplete world into a sharing in Christ's divine nature. The mystic extends this transfiguring liturgy through his actions. No matter how insignificant, banal, and monotonous his work may be, he is vibrantly aware of Jesus Christ, already glorified, living within him and working through him to bring the whole word to its fullness.

The mystic realizes, with St. Paul, that nothing can separate him from Christ. Christ is everything, and the contemplative finds Him everywhere. He realizes that everything now can unite him with Christ. "The heart rears wings bolder and bolder. And hurls for him, O Half hurls earth for him off under his feet."[4]

The false dichotomy between action and contemplation, between the profane and the sacred, ceases to exist, as a deeper consciousness of the abiding presence of the Trinity permeates the man of prayer. He seeks to trace the Holy Trinity in all of creature. It is not as though his action is done in a contemplative atmosphere, but rather that contemplation is perfected in an atmosphere of action. Contemplation flows from the fullness of one's activity, because one finds God in the very activity. He discovers the divine richness in the most commonplace action. He finds the Holy Trinity at work for the redemption of the human race and is himself an instrument of the application of divine redemption in the dramatic adventure of life.

The man of prayer does not seek a state of recollection in which, while standing in Grand Central Station absorbed in God, he can be ignorant of the crowd pressing all about him. His is a recollection by which he is absorbed in God and at the same time very much aware of the crowd, because he sees on each one in that crowd a brother and sister in Christ, actually or in potency through grace. He sees on each one the mark of the Sacred Blood of Jesus Christ. He sees in each soul the terrible conflict with the powers of hell that bind each person until Jesus Christ descends into that hell to heal and free him. For such a contemplative in action there is no insignificant event that does not bear the stamp of the Holy Trinity's desire to redeem all creation and restore it through Christ to the original plan as conceived by the Holy Trinity. Whatever such a person does by way of work, he is contemplating the Trinity, and his action proceeds precisely from this centering upon the Source of his being and that of the world's.

Such a transfiguring contemplation is based on the three infused gifts of the Holy Spirit: faith, hope and charity. Faith takes off the veil in creatures that hides the Face of God behind so many distortions. It points out the redemptive plan in every occurrence and in every human action, and gives everything its proper context in Christ. Faith shows God in all creatures and all creatures in God. Such a contemplative does not need to spend long hours in silent contemplation, far removed from human society. He finds God through the faith that tells him and aids him to find Christ Jesus in everything that moves and has being. Faith shows him the burning Heart of Christ, His overflowing love for all men, and precisely through such contemplation and no longer in spite of activity, Christ demands love in return, a service that extends to all men and wants to pour out His love to all.

Hope is a realization of one's nothingness and God's infinite allness and His infinite love for all. It is an opening up of self and a putting on of the potentialities of God, an abandoning of one's weakness to the almighty strength of Christ in order that one's actions, both little and great, may be done in Him and through His strength.

Charity purifies one's selfish desires to possess for oneself and makes oneself desire to give for Another, God. Charity is the receiving of God and the giving of self in union with Him through the action at hand, done with energy as a symbol of one's complete oblation to God, the tremendous Lover.

When stress and strain during action performed for God become so great, so distracting even, that it is impossible to center any actual attention on God, faith, hope and charity still make it possible to continue this contemplation of God in a virtual manner. There remains always a certain awareness of the present reality of God, a background music that never leaves us. Due to the circumstances of interaction with other creatures, the press of activities, one cannot attend with total consciousness to God's presence. Attention may be fixed on creatures that require our absorbing concentration, but through faith, hope, and charity, our attention is not centered on creatures as upon an ultimate concern, to use Paul Tillich's favorite phrase.

For the contemplative who moves always under the transfiguring light of Christ's presence, the spiritual aware- ness of God's presence and love is not competing for attention in opposition to distracting creatures but is the "milieu" in which these absorbing activities unfold. But to "see" God continually in every creature, in every action, to have a pure intention of glorifying God in all that we do, to be completely dedicated to loving God without any admixture of self-love ("purity of heart" as St. John Cassian describes it), to move and act out of love for God in the most worldly situations, to reveal the glory of God to all men, without detriment to the intimate union of the interior life or to continual prayer in the midst of unceasing activity, all this will remain an unrealizable ideal until God steps down and grants us, by His merciful intervention, an extraordinary grace.

Unless God grants us an infusion of faith, hope, and charity, permitting us to find Him in all things, there will always exist the dichotemy, a result of man's sinful alienation from God, between contemplation and action

PAN-EN-THEISM

It was St. Paul who first spoke of all things in God
and God in all things. "And when everything is subjected
to Him, then the Son Himself will be subjected in His turn
to the One who subjected all things to Him, so that God
may be all in all" (1 Cor. 15, 28).

But God's transparency is to be an illumination, not a
destruction of the created world. The creature contemplated is not a means, an instrument to lead us to God alone.
God is to be contemplated as the inner reality of His
world, as a loving gift.

I remember once having the experience of praying on
Mount Tabor and quite humorously being reminded of
Dietrich Bonhoeffer's words, "In Christ we are offered the
possibility of partaking in the reality of God and in the
reality of the world, but not in the one without the
other." I had taken the local bus, filled with Arabs from
Nazareth to the small Arab town below Mount Tabor. I
wanted to accompany on foot Jesus and His Disciples,
Peter, James and John, to the top. We had a wonderful
conversation up the winding road that after a mile
or so brought me to the beautiful Basilica of the Transfiguration. There kneeling in a church almost emptied
of tourists, I felt the exhilaration of Peter and the
other two before the Transfigured Jesus. "Lord, it
is wonderful for us to be here. . ." (Matt. 17,2). The
warm light of the Lord seemed to be a physical presence that engulfed me. This was it; real contemplation!
Then a buzz that sooned turned into a disturbing whine;
then an awful bite! The place was also a convention of
mosquitoes!

I wondered whether their ancestors also disturbed Peter, James and John in the midst of their ecstasy. It was easy to get God's message. The transfiguration takes place in a disturbing world, incomplete, sordid, sinful, yet God's world, the place He has wished to become incarnate for love of us and also to become transfigured!

God's presence becomes for the contemplative a light that is seen stretching *upwards*. The Apostles "looked up" and saw Jesus Christ and Moses and Elias transfigured on top of Mount Tabor. The movement of a person of deep prayer is from darkness towards the transcendent light of God's presence.

> Arise, shine out, for your light has come.
> the glory of Yahweh is rising on you,
> though night still covers the earth
> and darkness the peoples.
>
> Above you Yahweh now rises
> and above you His glory appears.
> The nations come to your light
> and kings to your dawning brightness.
>
> . . .At this sight you will grow radiant,
> your heart throbbing and full
> since the riches of the sea will flow to you,
> the wealth of the nations come to you;
>
> . . .No more will the sun give you daylight,
> nor moonlight shine on you,
> but Yahweh will be your everlasting light,
> your God will be your splendour.
>
> Your sun will set no more
> nor your moon wane,
> but Yahweh will be your everlasting light
> and your days of mourning will be ended.

> Your people will all be upright,
> possessing the land for ever;
> a shoot that Yahweh has planted,
> my handiwork, designed for beauty. (Is. 60, 1–21).

But the mystic, bathed in God's light, also becomes light. St. Paul writes: "You were darkness once, but now you are light in the Lord; be like children of light, for the effects of the light are seen in complete goodness and right living and truth. . .anything exposed by the light will be illuminated and anything illuminated turns into light. That is why it is said:

> Wake up from your sleep,
> rise from the dead,
> and Christ will shine on you." (Ephes. 5:8–14).

Christ is the transfiguring light that radiates from within. He is the life that is "the light of men" (Jn. 1,4). This Divine Word is incessantly being spoken by the Heavenly Father within us; this Word is "the true light that enlightens all men" (Jn. 1, 9). Jesus Himself tells us: "I am the light of the world; anyone who follows me will not be walking in the dark, he will have the light of life" (Jn. 8, 12). Sharing in His light, we too "are the light of the world. . .In the same way your light must shine in the sight of men, so that, seeing your good works, they may give the praise to your Father in heaven" (Matt. 5:14–16).

　-　We look up to see Jesus Christ transfigured on the mountain. We also look downward—downward into our own being and downward into the world. We understand by God's light that the world comes from Him and leads us to His inner presence within His evolving world. God draws the contemplative to an immediacy that cannot ignore the world and human beings. Rather, focused totally upon God by His strong attraction of love, we are gradually freed from all self-centeredness in order to be able to love human beings with a more universal, more purified love. "Blessed are the pure in heart, for they shall see God" in the whole universe.

The contemplative looks down into God's uncompleted world, the world that He is still creating with man's cooperation. The person of prayer is much like Mary, the Mother of God, as she entered into the cave at Bethlehem. It surely was not the idealized cave of Italian religious art or popular Christmas cards. Mary brought forth Jesus and laid Him in a manger of straw. We know what straw in a cave that had laid there for months, perhaps even years. It had become dank, full of cob-webs and the mute inhabitation of other crawling bugs, spiders and other despised creatures of this world. A dusty cave where the dung of animals who slept there during the long winter nights had accumulated over weeks and months and perhaps years.

This was the real world into which God was entering to begin His transfiguring process. It was His world, real and unfinished. Christ as a newly born child was stripped of everything as a sign of what was to come. He was the mustard seed, so insignificant, yet from it would come the huge tree that would harbor the birds of the air. The process of re-creation was beginning. The evolution of the People of God and the transfiguration of the universe was beginning with this *Proton* of Divine Love. Here we see the utter simplicity, the monad of divinity beginning with a spark of humanity. Nothing else. Mary and Joseph meet "raw" nature. Nothing of the technical world around. From such a simple, ordinary beginning, God would manifest His great love for us.

In contemplation, therefore, God calls us downward to His suffering world. Once we experience in prayer the transfiguring power of God's love for us, we can love His world by surrendering ourselves to His presence in order to serve and to bring Him forth more radiantly and more explicitly, so that the whole world may recognize that He is the source of all being. In discovering God at our center, we discover Him also as the center of His world. Rooted in God, we can go forth and love the world as God loves it. We move at each moment from light to greater light, from God to God in all things.

Heaven has begun even on this earth. We have died to self and have already risen with Christ. We have put on the thoughts of things above, because we have now already begun to glimpse the reality that, as St. Paul says, Jesus Christ is in all things. The Heavenly Jerusalem is now piercing through the suffering shadows of a world that is still groaning before it is brought into the full life already glimpsed as present. For the mystic, looking up to the transfigured Jesus and down to the suffering Lord,

> The throne of God and of the Lamb will be in its
> place in the city.
> His servants will worship Him.
> They will see Him face to face
> and His name will be written on their foreheads.
> It will never be night again and they will not
> need lamplight or sunlight, because the Lord God
> will be shining on them.
> They will reign for ever and ever (Rev. 22:3–5).

FOOTNOTES

Introduction

[1] Julian Green's *Journal,* Tomes 1–7 (1928-1958; Plon), p. 439

[2] Kahlil Gibran: *The Prophet* (N.Y. 1969), p. 69.

[3] Evelyn Underhill: *The School of Charity and the Mystery of Sacrifice* (N.Y. Longmans, Green and Co., 1956), p. 235.

[4] Pseudo-Dionysius: Mystical Theology, 1.

[5] Cf. Allan Lewis: "The Theatre and the Revolt Against Reason," in *Conversations "72"* (Garrison, New York: 1972), pp. 16–19.

Chapter 1

[1] Charles Peguy. *Eve* (Paris, ed. La Pleiade; 1941) pg. 764.

[2] C. S. Lewis: *Letters to Malcolm*; (N.Y. Harcourt, Brace and World, 1964) p. 84.

[3] T. Merton: *Contemplative Prayer* (N.Y. 1970) p. 112.

[4] J. Ruysbroeck: *Mirror of Eternal Salvation* (London, 1946) p. 73.

[5] *John of the Cross: Complete Works,* Tr. by Peers, E. Allison (Newman, Westminster, Md. 1946), Bk. II, viii, Vol. I, pg. 420.

[6] *The Complete Works of Saint Teresa of Jesus;* E. Allison Peers, tr and ed. (Sheed & Ward, N.Y. 1946); Vol. II, VII *Mansions,* pp. 331–332.

[7] *Hymn to Jesus Christ, XIII;* translation my own.

Chapter 2

[1]T. Merton, *The Climate of Monastic Prayer* (Cistercian Publications, Spencer, Mass., 1968), p. 147.

Chapter 3

I. Hausherr: Les lecons *d'un Contemplatif. Le Traité de l'Oraison d'Evagre le Pontique* (Paris, 1960), pp. 76–8.

[2]*De Fide Orthodoxa;* Bk. 50; 4: PG. 94, 800B.

[3]*Song of Songs;* PG. 44, 10000D, quoted from *Glory to Glory,* p. 247; ed. by J. Danielou and H. Musurillo (Scribner, N.Y., 1961).

[4]Cf. L. Bouyer: *The Spirituality of the New Testament and the Fathers* (Désclée, N.Y., 1960), p. 356.

[5]Cf. Comm. on *Song of Songs;* PG. 44, 893B, cited by Danielou in *From Glory to Glory, op. cit.,* p. 32.

[6]V. Lossky: *Vision of God* (Faith Press, Clayton, Wisc., 1963), pp. 71, 74

[7]*Comm. on Song of Songs;* PG. 44, 1001B.

[8]*Life of Moses,* 376C–377A, cited in *From Glory to Glory,* p. 118.

[9]Gregory of Nyssa: *On Perfection,* tr. by Virginia Woods Callahan; in *Ascetical Works of Gregory of Nyssa; Fathers of the Church;* Vol. 58 (Wash., D.C., 1967), p. 122.

[10]*Life of Moses,* cited in *From Glory to Glory, op. cit.,* p. 144.

[11]*Ibid.,* p. 148.

[12]*Commentary on Song of Songs;* cited *From Glory to Glory,* p. 270

13*Ibid.*

14*Life of Moses;* PG. 44, 301C; cited *Fr m Glory to Glory*, p. 83.

15*Ibid.,* p. 149.

16*Ibid.,* p. 144.

Chapter 5

1 By Richard Bach (Mac Millan Co., 1970).

2*Ibid.,* pp. 90–91.

3 Emil Brunner, *Man in Revolt* (London, 1953), pp. 97–98.

4 A. Festugiere, *Contemplation et vie contemplative chez Platon,* Part II, p. 288.

5 De Beatitudine I, *PG.* 44, 1196.

6 Hom. in Ps. 61, *PG.* 29, 476C, 477A.

7 Hom. in Ps. 33, 7, *PG.* 29, 268B.

8 Letter to the Romans, 5, in: *Fathers of the Church* Series, Vol. 1, (Washington, D.C., 1946), p. 110.

9*De perfecta Christiani forma, PG.* 46, 251–256.

10*De perfecta Christiani forma,* PG. 46, 251–256.

11*De Spiritu Sancto,* 16, *PG.* 32, 140B.

12*Enchiridion Patristicum,* no. 780, 782.

13*Comment. in Joan,* IV, I, *PG.* 74, 316A.

[14]Cf. I. Hausherr, S. J., "Dogme et spiritualite orientale," in *Revue d'ascetique et mystique* (1947), pp. 31–33.

[15]*Ad. Olypium monachum, PG.* 46, 256B.

[16]*Adv. oppugn. vitae monasticae,* III, 15; *PG.* 47, 372.

[17]II *Contra Arianos* 59; *PG.* XXVI, 273.

[18]II Pet. 1, 4.

[19]*Ambigua; PG. XCI, 1076C.*

[20]*Ibid,* 1308 b.

[21]*Gen.* 1, 26.

[22]*Theatetes,* 176 b.

[23]*Haer. Lib.* III, t. 1; PG XLII, 341–345.

[24]*Adv. Haer. Liber* V; PG. VII, 1138.

[25]*Sermo Asceticus;* PG. LXXIX, 1281 d.

[26]*Epistola* II; PG. XXXIV, 413 c, 412 c.

[27]Cf: *supra,* ftnote 17.

[28]H. Crouzel, S. J.: *Théologie de l'image de Dieu chez Origene* (Paris, 1956).

Chapter 6

[1]*Christologie et Evolution* (Paris, 1933), pp. 11–12.

[2]C. T. Wood: *The Life, Letters and Religion of St. Paul* (Edinburgh, Clark, 1925), p. 320.

3Cf. V. Lossky: *The Mystical Theology of the Eastern Church* (London, 1968), p. 98.

4Polycarp Sherwood: *The Earlier Ambigua of St. Maximus the Confessor* (Rome, 1955), p. 176.

5Maximus: *Ambigua;* PG. 91, 1308, cited by Lossky, *op. cit.,* p. 214.

6Cf. Pegon, J.: *Centuries sur la Charite de S. Maxime Le Confesseur;* in *Sources Chretiennes,* 9 (Paris, Editions du Cerf, 1943), p. 54.

7*The Four Centuries on Charity;* in: *Ancient Christian Writers,* 21 (Estminister, Md., Newman Press, 1955), II, 48; p. 162.

8Cf. my treatment of Maximus' contemplation in *The Cosmic Christ* (Sheed & Ward, N.Y. 1968), pp. 167–78.

9This section on the five divisions is based on Thunberg's development in his: *Microcosm and Mediator: The Theological Anthropology of Maximus the Confessor* (Copenhagen, Lund, 1965).

10*Ambigua;* PG. 91, 1308B, cited in Lossky, *op. cit.,* p. 126.

11*Mystagogia;* PG. 91, 665–668.

12Cf. *Ad Thallasium,* PG. 90, 63; 673C.

13*Ambigua* 5, PG. 91, 1060A.

14Cf. V. Lossky, *op. cit.,* p. 146.

Chapter 7

1Cf. M. L. Gardet: "La mention du nom divine en mystique musulmane," in: *Revue Thomiste* (1952), pp. 642–646; also, "La technique hindoue de la meditation," in: *Etudes Carmelitaines: Technique et Contemplation* (Paris, 1949), pp. 17–35.

[2]Homilia 90 in Evang. S. Matthaei, 15, 3.

[3]Evagrius: De Oratione; PG. LXXIX, 1168D.

[4]*Life of Antony,* Post-Nicene Fathers, 2nd Ser., 4 (Grand Rapids, 1957), p. 214.

[5]P. Tillich, "The Eternal Now," in *The Modern Vision of Death,* ed. N. A. Scott, Jr. (Richmond, Va., 1967), p. 103.

[6]A saying attributed to Abbot Poemen. *Apophthegmata Patrum,* P.G., 65, 353A.

[7]Climacus (Step 7), p. 114.

Chapter 8

[1]Nil Sorsky, *Ustav,* pg. 28 (from the critical text of M. A. Borov-kova-Maikova: Nila Sorskago Predanie i Ustav s vsupital 'noi stat' ei; in: Pamiatniki drevnei mennosti, no. 179, St. Petersburg, 1912. Translation my own. For a detailed work on Nil's spirituality, cf: G. A. Maloney, S. J.: *Russian Hesychasm: The Spirituality of Nil Sorsky* (Mouton, the Hague, (1973).

[2]Simeon the New Theologian: *Divinorum amorum Liber,* Hymn 13, pg. 120, 526 c-d.

[3]Maisie Ward: *The Divine Eccentric* (London, 1943), pg. 74.

[4]G. M. Hopkins: "Hurrahing in Harvest," in: *Poems of Gerard M. Hopkins,* by W. H. Gardner and N. H. MacKenzie, 4th ed. (London, Oxford Press, 1967) p. 70.